IRISH
IMMIGRANTS
— *in* —
MICHIGAN
· A History in Stories ·

Pat Commins & Elizabeth Rice

THE
History
PRESS

For Lucy and Teddy,
Happy Reading,
Elizabeth Rice
Pat Commins
2021

Published by The History Press
Charleston, SC
www.historypress.com

Maps of counties in Ireland and Michigan featured on pages 12 and 13 are artist's renderings courtesy of Tricksy Wizard Comics.

First published 2021

Manufactured in the United States

ISBN 9781467146319

Library of Congress Control Number: 2020945859

To Catherine, Denise and Geraldine, the keepers of memories.

CONTENTS

CONTENTS

ACKNOWLEDGEMENTS

Our thanks to The History Press and editor John Rodrigue for supporting us. We also wish to thank Dorothy Mallory, Ellen Buysse, Dr. Jane Rice and Tommy Commins for special contributions; Erin and Adam Rice-Carlson, artists of Tricksy Wizard Comics; David Gutierrez at Triple Axis Media Group; Deirdre Jones for sharing her expertise; and Dr. Aidan Sprague-Rice and Molly Sprague-Rice for offering listening ears and helpful advice. We are indebted to the librarians, archivists and members of historical societies for their assistance and patience in answering our queries. Especially, we thank our families and friends who have been so encouraging and supportive throughout this endeavor. WBSFA

COUNTIES OF IRELAND

COUNTIES OF MICHIGAN

INTRODUCTION

In cemeteries throughout Michigan, there are thousands of headstones with the names of Irish immigrants and their descendants. Some of the headstones are well preserved, while others are weatherworn and broken. When and why did these Irish immigrants come to Michigan? What inspired them to leave their homeland to travel across the Atlantic Ocean in a sailing ship? The reasons are many. By the nineteenth century, Ireland had been under the rule of England for centuries. Penal Laws established by Parliament in the seventeenth century forbade civil rights of land ownership, education, religious freedom, marriage and occupation for Irish Roman Catholics and others who dissented from the Church of England. The Penal Laws resulted in lives of poverty, destitution and hopelessness for most of the Irish population. Emigration seemed the only way out from such a life.

Prior to 1830, only those of financial means had the option to emigrate from Ireland. Most of these emigrants were from the northern Irish counties, followers of the Presbyterian Church, who, in general, fared better than their Catholic neighbors. The situation changed when the blight on the potato occurred. The potato was the staple food of Catholic tenant farmers and laborers in Ireland. From 1845 to 1850, the potato crop was infected with a fungal pathogen that ruined the harvest each year. The English government was slow to do anything about the increasing number of hungry, then starving, people. At the time, it was thought that relief efforts would encourage dependency on the government. Some officials promoted the idea that Divine Providence was at work, and so the government must not interfere.

More than one million people died in Ireland due to the potato famine (An Gorta Mor) between 1846 and 1851. Those who could booked passage on a ship leaving Ireland. Securing passage, however, was no guarantee that a person's troubles were over. Ships were overcrowded. A ship that boasted two hundred first- and second-class accommodations might also carry hundreds in third class, below deck, in steerage. Cholera and typhus claimed lives every day. Thousands died attempting the ocean crossing, which could last more than five weeks. Still, over one million people emigrated from Ireland during the worst of the famine.

Immigrant ships landed on the East Coast of the United States or in Quebec, Canada. Immigrants generally arrived in New York City, Boston, Philadelphia or Quebec City. Their first priorities were finding shelter and employment. These cities were already crowded. Housing was difficult to find. Jobs paid just enough to get through the day. Many immigrants remained in the big cities. Others headed west.

The Northwest Territory came into the possession of the United States in 1797. The Michigan Territory, in the northern region, was established in 1805. Numerous treaties with the indigenous people in the territory resulted in millions of acres of land ceded and available for settlement. When Michigan became a state in 1837, the government commenced surveys and geological reports of the resources in the state, thinking this would spur settlement. Michigan had abundant timber and mineral resources. The fur trade was thriving. Fish were plentiful.

The thousands of Michigan Irish immigrants became loggers, miners, fishermen, fur traders, rail workers, farmers, merchants, doctors, lawyers, pharmacists, soldiers and teachers. They and their children became part of Michigan's early state history. These stories offer a window into their daily lives: the hours of backbreaking work, the tragedies that befell them, their perseverance against all odds, glimpses of hope and humor. The stories also shed light on the social, political, economic, religious and cultural issues that are part of Michigan's history too.

The state of Michigan comprises eighty-three counties. This book comprises eighty-three Irish immigrant stories, one from each county. Some stories are about one person's life or one family's story. Others are about a community. Every story is true. Some are about people who can be found in history texts. Most are about people who were not famous except possibly in their own families. The stories are a testimony to all of the Irish who braved the ocean crossing in hopes of finding a better life.

Discrepancies of names, places, dates and events may have occurred, as sources sometimes differed and primary sources were not always available or accessible.

1

ALCONA COUNTY

A Mother Searches for Her Son

Mary Ann Moore was born in Ireland on March 17, 1826. She immigrated to Simcoe County, Ontario, while still a young girl. She married Alex Clark, who had emigrated from Scotland. Together, Mary Ann and Alex cleared land in order to begin farming. Twenty years later, Mary Ann was widowed. She found herself with ten children to raise and support. There were five boys and five girls.

Mary Ann did not have the means to support her family. She managed to keep some of the children with her on the farm. The others were placed with neighboring families. Mary Ann hoped that her "away" children would be well cared for. She hired herself out as a worker, taking whatever jobs she could find, in hopes of keeping her remaining children with her.

Mary Ann's youngest child, a son, was just a baby during this time of upheaval. He was placed with a family by the name of McRae. The McRaes operated a hotel in Goderich, Ontario, near the shore of Lake Huron. Mary Ann convinced herself that her baby was in good hands and would be well cared for. She was able to visit him sometimes.

One day, when Mary Ann journeyed to Goderich to see her baby, the McRaes were gone. No one knew where they had moved. Mary Ann's little boy was with them. She returned home with a heavy heart.

Several years later, Mary Ann was employed as a cook on lake vessels traveling on Lake Huron. One day, Mary Ann overheard someone speaking of a family named McRae who had traveled from Canada, settling in northeastern Michigan. With guarded hope, Mary Ann made a plan to find this family and her youngest son once again.

Three of Mary Ann's other sons traveled with her on a shore steamer called the *Flora*. The boat steamed north on Lake Huron, stopping at the town of Harrisville in Alcona County. Mary Ann and her sons disembarked. Immediately, Mary Ann's sons began looking for work.

It was a time of great lumbering in this part of Michigan. The brothers went to one of the lumber camps of Curley Jim Johnson in Haynes Township. The boys were not hefty enough for the grueling work required of lumbermen so they moved on to another camp run by the Pratt and Millen Company. They were hired to take out cut timber and lay ties for a narrow-gauge railroad needed to haul the timber to the town of Alcona. The brothers worked for Pratt and Millen for two seasons. Following this, they hired on to supply the wood fuel needed to run the new locomotives that recently had come to the area. The railway line, built in 1885, was Alcona County's first direct connection with other towns along the Lake Huron lakeshore and beyond.

The Clarks bought eighty acres of land from the Black River, Alger, Smith and Company for five dollars per acre. The company agreed to buy the fuel wood the brothers would provide. Mary Ann moved with her sons onto the property. The brothers piled their cut wood alongside the rail tracks that cut through their farm. They were paid one dollar per cord of wood. The wood was cut in two-foot lengths, stacked six feet high. The stacks were separated by a length of wood so that a passing inspector could see that they were the desired length and height.

Mary Ann lived with her sons until her death in 1913. She never received any news of her youngest boy, but she never forgot him. In a time of great hardship and heartache, Mary Ann worked tirelessly to keep her family together. It was not possible for her to keep all of her children united under one roof, so she made difficult decisions in what she felt to be the children's best interests: tending to those she could, placing some with other families and searching throughout her lifetime for one who disappeared.

2
ALGER COUNTY

From Saloonkeeper to Sheriff

Patrick Mulconry immigrated to New York from County Clare, Ireland. When Patrick stepped off the ship, he was fortunate to find work on a farm in Oneida County. From there, Patrick moved to Westchester County, where he met and married Sarah Miller. Their son, James, was born on May 2, 1851, the second child born to them. Eventually, nine more children followed. James lived on the family farm until he was sixteen years old.

Patrick left farm work when he became employed by the New York and Hudson Railway Company. James saw this as his opportunity to go west and traveled to Illinois. He found work on a farm in La Salle Township, Illinois. After four years, James traveled to Montcalm, Michigan. He had heard about work in sawmills that paid much higher wages than farm labor. The lumber boom was on in Michigan, and James wanted to be a part of it. James saved all of the money that he could, as he had aspirations beyond the grueling work of a lumberman. With his savings, James left lumbering. He entered the retail liquor business and opened his first saloon in Edmore, Michigan, in 1877.

During this year, James married Minnie Townsend. Minnie had come from Steuben County, New York. She and James had three children. James ran the saloon in Edmore for fourteen years. Ready for a new adventure, he moved his family to Ewen Township in Ontonagon County in the Western Upper Peninsula, where he continued as a saloonkeeper for a number of years. Eventually, he felt called to move again, this time to Munising, in Alger County. There seemed to always be room for another saloonkeeper, so once more, James opened a drinking establishment. The saloon was a success, as most saloons were not only watering holes but also important meeting places for the lumbermen, farmers and laborers of the community. Politicians knew that to get a finger on the pulse of their constituency, the place to be was a local saloon. The political issues of the day, as well as the social, religious and economic issues uppermost in people's minds, were all discussed there.

As the saloonkeeper, James was well placed to hear about all of these issues. He knew most of the 5,868 residents of Alger County. He also provided a listening ear to anyone who confided in him. Thus, James's name came up as a potential candidate for sheriff in Alger County. Counties were governed by established customs, traditions and partisan politics. A sheriff did not need a formal education or any law enforcement training. A sheriff did not answer to anyone during his four years' tenure. Accountability came only at election time when those who had the right to vote cast their ballots.

The year was 1908. Minnie died in 1906. James decided to sell his saloon and run for the position of sheriff. He had married for the second time earlier in the year to a woman named Pauline Ryan. Just like James, Pauline was the daughter of Irish immigrants. In November, James Mulconry was voted in as the sheriff of the county and served in that role for the next four years. His commendation after his term of service read, "He has given a most careful and punctilious administration of the shrievalty and through his services has admirably conserved law and order, the while he has been successful in the apprehension of a number of notorious malefactors."

From saloonkeeper to sheriff, James Mulconry left his mark in Alger County.

3

ALLEGAN COUNTY

A Place of His Own

In the 1800s, tenant farmers in Ireland lived precariously from day to day. Most were barely able to provide for their families on their small plots of rented land. The custom was to subdivide the land as sons grew to manhood, but this tradition led to tenant farms of ever decreasing size. When the potato blights occurred, that once plentiful source of food was taken away as well. Landlords began to see the economic advantage of grazing cattle versus waiting for their tenants to scrape together their yearly rents. Cattle prices were increasing. Landlords could make much higher profits from grazing the land. Evictions occurred. For many poor Irish people, their only hope lay in emigrating. The word was out that America was the place where a poor man could begin again with land and work aplenty.

James Graham was born in the parish of Kilglass, in County Sligo, in 1830. His father, William, was a tenant farmer, barely able to maintain a living standard above abject poverty. There was no hope of a better life for James in Ireland. The family farm would go to James's elder brother, Edward. In 1847, when James was seventeen years old, he made the choice to emigrate. County Sligo saw so many emigrations in the nineteenth century that it was common to sail directly from Sligo to New York, Boston, Quebec or St. John's, Newfoundland. The fare to Canada was less than the fare to the United States, so many of the poorest traveled there. James somehow found the means to book his passage to Canada.

After his arrival in Canada, James soon found employment. He remained in Canada for two years, then headed for the state of New York. He found work in a sawmill, holding his position there for eight years. During this time, James married Catherine Fuller. The Grahams remained in New York for six more years. In 1853, the family traveled directly to Allegan County, Michigan. They had heard about the plentiful and affordable land waiting to be claimed there. James used the family savings to purchase 160 acres of land in Cheshire Township. The land was a wilderness. There were no roads, only forest and shrubs.

The first priority was to get a house built. With a roof over their heads, the family could turn to clearing the forest land. Seventeen years later, the 1880 census recorded that James Graham owned 190 acres of land, 110 of which were forested, 35 were arable for farming and 4 were planted in apple trees. All of the work was done by the family on their own. The oldest son, John, bred draft horses for use on the farm.

In time, James and Catherine became prominent, respected members of the Cheshire Township community. James was a deacon and trustee of the local Baptist church as well as a Sunday school teacher. He was an assessor for the Allegan County school district for twelve years. Notably, James was instrumental in the drainage of Cheshire Township, which opened up more land to farming pursuits and the expansion of the township. The dream of a place of his own eluded James Graham back in County Sligo but became a reality in Allegan County, Michigan.

4

ALPENA COUNTY

Growing a County

James and Jennette Austin Davison lived near the town of Larne in County Antrim, Ireland. They decided to immigrate to America in 1841 with their young son. When they reached New York, the family traveled west to Lenawee County in Michigan. Jennette gave birth to a son, Samuel, on November 18, 1841. The family left Lenawee County and moved to Otisville, a small village in Forest Township, in Genesee County. James's uncle, William Davison, was living there. He owned eighty acres of land. James worked with his uncle for many years clearing the land. During this time, five more children were born into the family. In 1854, James died at the age of fifty-two, leaving Jennette and seven children. Samuel, aged thirteen, hired himself out for farming and lumbering jobs to support the family for the next sixteen years.

At the age of twenty-nine, Samuel left the family home. He headed north, where lumbering was going on in a big way. In 1870, Samuel made his first visit to Alpena County. He wanted to invest in the timber forests and land in general. He began to buy land, which he then cleared and sold to new settlers. Over the next ten years, Samuel built up a very successful business. He advertised the benefits of Alpena County to immigrants looking for a place to settle. He advertised in southern Michigan, Canadian port towns and the eastern states. His advertisements described all of the advantages and opportunities immigrants would find in the county.

In 1879, Samuel returned to Otisville so that he and Mary Jane Henderson could marry. The following year, they moved to Alpena County. They lived on land that Samuel planned to clear for a farm. Here they would raise their family. The family remained on the farm until the year 1888, when Samuel decided to move into the town of Alpena with Mary Jane and their three children. Mary Jane was not well. She died three years later at the age of thirty-eight, in October 1891.

Three years after Mary Jane's death, Samuel remarried. His second wife was Lowida Richmond, a native of Oakland County, Michigan, and formerly the matron of the School for the Deaf in Flint, Michigan. Samuel continued buying land, clearing it and dividing it into small plots, which he sold to new settlers coming into the county. Samuel sold the small plots of land at prices people could afford. He believed strongly that once forested land had the potential to become excellent farmland. Samuel explained to prospective buyers that their new land was well suited for wheat, corn, hay and potatoes.

In 1896, Samuel decided to expand his business opportunities by purchasing a shingle mill. He bought the Warren Davis Shingle Mill and began operations. Running at full capacity, the mill produced forty thousand shingles per day. Samuel employed one hundred men. The mill also sold other lumber products. Samuel became an investor in two local lumber companies, the Kimball Lumber Company and the Churchill Lumber Company. He was also appointed a director of both the Alpena National Bank and the Alpena County Savings Bank. Samuel Davison was known as one of Alpena's most influential residents. He was respected by everyone in the community.

As the twentieth century began, Samuel lessened the number of hours he devoted to his business operations. He suffered from bouts of ill health and decided to retire. His wife, Lowida, survived an operation for appendicitis but then passed away from peritonitis one week later on December 27, 1914. Samuel fell and broke a hip in May 1918. His mobility curtailed, he was no longer seen around the town. A second fall occurred later that year, which caused his healing hip to break again. Surrounded by his children, Samuel passed away on August 5, 1918. He was one of the true growers of the county, demonstrated by the large numbers of immigrants he had persuaded to settle in Alpena.

5

ANTRIM COUNTY

A Man for His Adopted Country

John Keefe was a native of Dublin. He was born on December 28, 1826, and only two years old when his parents passed away. John was placed with different families during his youth. Most of this time, he was living in homes on various farms in the Irish countryside.

When John was twelve years old, he made up his mind to travel to America. He had saved four pounds and fifteen shillings—enough to book passage from Ireland to Boston, Massachusetts. On board the ship, John made himself known and helpful to the crew. The sailors paid John for assisting them in their tasks. He also helped the cook and carried messages for passengers. By the time he reached Boston, he had nearly earned the cost of his passage back again.

Arriving in Boston, John found work as a cook aboard a ship traveling up and down the East Coast. This job lasted for one year. Afterward, John found another position on a different vessel, this one sailing along the Atlantic and Gulf coasts and even to Europe. By the age of fifteen, he had already traveled back and forth across the Atlantic Ocean and visited Greece and other Mediterranean ports. Eighteen months later, coming into the harbor at Portsmouth, New Hampshire, the ship crashed, and many of the sailors were badly injured. John decided that he had had enough of the sea and made his way to Bangor, Maine.

In Bangor, John met a fellow Irishman from Belfast. The man took John into his home and treated him like one of his own sons. While living in Rockland, near Bangor, John learned the trade of stonecutting. He soon

CIVIL WAR RECRUITING

ALTHOUGH THERE WAS NO LARGE SCALE ORGANIZED ARMY DRAFT UNTIL WORLD WAR I,
MANY MEASURES WERE TAKEN TO RECRUIT MEN FOR THE SERVICE. FRANK LESLIE, THE
FAMOUS ILLUSTRATOR HAS LEFT THIS MEMENTO OF THE CIVIL WAR.

Civil War recruitment poster. *Michigan State University Archives and Historical Collections.*

became proficient, and his services were much in demand. John worked as a stonecutter for nearly twenty years.

When the American Civil War began, John enlisted in the Union army on May 7, 1861, in Company H, Fourth Maine Infantry. His regiment was part of the Army of the Potomac under General Ward. For his gallantry and service, John was promoted to picket sergeant, one of two, along with a lieutenant, four corporals and forty men of the regiment, who acted as an advance guard for the main army. He participated in many battles, suffering numerous injuries and wounds during his four years of service.

John came to be the bearer of a battle flag that had been sewn by some women of New York. The flag was carried at the front of every advance, serving to encourage the men following behind it. During one battle, the regular flag bearer was shot and killed. The flag fell to the ground. John swooped in to pick up the flag and held it aloft at the front of the line as he and his regiment advanced. As a testimony to his bravery, John was presented with a beautifully sewn flag, five feet by ten feet in length. He carried the flag with him when he was honorably discharged on July 19, 1864.

John heard about the land and natural resources of northern Michigan. With his wife and children, he traveled to Michigan, arriving in Antrim County in November 1865. He was able to procure land for a homestead near Torch Lake. His days were spent clearing land for a farm and building a home for his family. When the first town meeting was held in Eastport, Michigan, in 1866, John was one of the thirteen men present. John carried his flag with him to the meeting.

Once the farm and house were built, John hired himself out as a laborer for other farmers. His wife and children managed their farm. By hiring out, John earned one dollar per day. Often, he walked more than twenty miles to work. After his day's work, he walked back home, saw his family, slept, then began the long walk again early the next day.

The story of John Keefe moves from tragedy to confidence to courage. Leaving his home country led him to his adopted country.

6
ARENAC COUNTY

Following the Lumber Trail

Patrick Joseph McLean was born on July 1, 1850, to Patrick and Mary Ann McLean. His parents emigrated from Queenstown, the city of Cork, in Ireland. They landed in Simcoe County, Ontario, along with hundreds of other Irish immigrants. The passage from Ireland to ports in Canada was less expensive than sailing to the United States. Patrick was born in the town of Mara in Ontario.

When Patrick was old enough to strike out on his own, he found wintertime work in lumber camps. During the summertime, he worked on the family farm. At the age of twenty-seven, Patrick married Susan Cuddahee on August 26, 1877.

Patrick and Susan remained in Mara for five years. During this time, Susan gave birth to two sons. Thinking of his growing family, Patrick felt encouraged to head to Michigan for lumber work, having heard the trees were too numerous to count. Patrick's friend John Shay was also determined to get to Michigan. Patrick and John left Mara with a team of horses and a wagon. They journeyed to Cleveland, Ohio, where they found work. Patrick planned to save his earnings in order to eventually buy land in Michigan. With steady work, he sent for Susan and his two boys. The family lived in Cleveland for three years, and two more sons were born into the family.

Finally, the day came for Patrick and his family to move to Michigan. The McLeans traveled to Bay City, a lumber and port town. Bay City was thriving with lake vessels entering the bay and then leaving loaded with lumber and goods destined for other port cities and beyond. For two years,

Horse-drawn lumber train. *Michigan Technological University Archives and Copper Country Collections.*

the McLeans lived here until Patrick heard about the "Old Camps" in Sims Township, near Au Gres, in Arenac County, farther north along the Lake Huron shoreline. Once again, the family moved, following the lumber work. Patrick continued working in the lumber camps in the wintertime. In the summertime, he worked as a carpenter. Within a few years, Patrick had become a foreman of the Cole and Grimore Lumbering Company. This position allowed Patrick to save enough money in order to buy eighty acres of densely wooded land.

Here, on their own parcel of land, the family began the arduous job of clearing the trees in order to put up a log cabin, four rooms in size. More clearing of trees allowed for their first planting of crops, followed by obtaining a few head of cattle. Everyone pitched in to enlarge their planting and grazing areas. Sadly, Patrick's youngest son, William, died at the age of eleven. The McLeans bore their heavy loss by keeping on with their daily work and took solace from their religious faith. The McLeans were one of the first Catholic families to come to Au Gres. In 1895, Patrick, with others, helped to build the Catholic church known as St. Mark's.

Patrick was a talented musician. He played the violin and was much in demand at social gatherings and parties. At the end of the night, he was paid three dollars. Sometimes, the gatherings continued all through the night. Music brought everyone together, providing a bit of lightheartedness to break up the long hours of hard work endured every day.

Following the lumber trail from Canada to Michigan brought the McLean family, now numbering eight sons and three daughters, to Arenac County. Patrick's parents had sailed from Ireland in order to provide their children the opportunity for a better life. Patrick and Susan McLean carried on the torch passed to them to provide the same for their children.

7

BARAGA COUNTY

The Famine and Families

The year 1847 was a deadly one in Ireland, with the potato crop devastated by fungus and families devastated by starvation. Those who could scrape together enough money for the passage to Canada or the United States made their way to ports. Rarely was there enough money for an entire family to make the journey. Difficult decisions had to be made. Who would go, and who would stay? Many families discussed sending the most able member, who would find work and lodging and then save enough money to send for the rest of the family. The reality was that often there was never enough money, and most who sailed never saw their family in Ireland again.

Michael and Catherine Sheedy McMahan and their family of six children had to make this hard decision. It seemed there was no way that the family could remain together and survive. It was decided that the four boys in the family would sail to America. The two girls and the parents would remain in Ennis, County Clare, Ireland. The sons—Michael, Thomas, John and Simon—boarded a ship and made the crossing in eighteen days. They were fortunate. Often, the voyage lasted six weeks.

Upon the brothers' arrival in New York, the older three settled in Broom County. Simon, the youngest, found work on the New York and Erie Railroad, which was under construction. Simon became an engineer in the company. Eventually, he moved to Port Huron, Michigan. Simon married Johanna O'Rourke, herself an immigrant from Ballyneety, County Limerick, Ireland. Johanna had arrived in the United States at the young age of twelve. Their son James was born in Port Huron. Eventually, nine more children joined the family.

When James was eight years old, the family moved to Midland County in Michigan. Simon bought a farm, and everyone worked together to make it a success. The children were able to attend a local school. James remained with his family until his eighteenth birthday. He then left home and found work as a fireman on the railroad. The work was hard, physical labor. The firemen shoveled fuel into the boiler firebox to keep the trains running. Two years later, James left the railroad company. He traveled to Saginaw and became a lumberjack. He also found work in the Saginaw Barrel factory. While James lived in Saginaw, news of his father's death reached him. James did not return to Midland; he remained in Saginaw for another two years. At twenty-two years old, though, James was ready for new adventures.

In 1884, there were many opportunities for lumbering in Michigan's Northern Peninsula. James settled in Baraga Township in Baraga County. He found work in lumbering and in the saloon business. In 1886, James met and married Annie Auge. Together, they became parents to eight children. Baraga County was a wilderness still, though the area was expanding rapidly. There were only a few houses in the area where James lived with his family.

The saloon business was quite profitable. It was not long before James McMahon became a well-known and respected businessperson in the county.

Log decks. *Michigan State University Archives and Historical Collections.*

He was appointed postmaster, a position he held for seven years. James also served as the county treasurer, the township clerk and the justice of the peace. His own interests led him to politics and into the real estate business.

In 1901, the death of the sitting probate county judge caused a vacancy in Baraga County. James McMahan was elected to fill the post for two years. He settled estates and executed wills; his knowledge of the area, gained from his real estate dealings, encouraged people to trust in him. He was reelected twice. The sacrifice of James's Irish grandparents, sending his father and uncles to America, enabled James and his family to realize lives free from hunger and want.

8

BARRY COUNTY

A Farmer at Heart

Skryne is a lush agricultural area located in County Meath, Ireland. The land lies within sight of the royal palace of Ireland's ancient high kings. Matthew Mulvaney was born here in 1796. His wife, Margaret Boyle, was born in 1799. In 1828, Matthew and Margaret left Ireland with their two sons, Peter and three-year-old James. The family traveled to Dublin, where they boarded the *Duncan Gib* for Quebec. After a voyage of five weeks and three days, they arrived. Matthew was nearly penniless but determined to find work. He managed to get employment in Brookville, Ontario. After saving some money, he made his way alone to Salina, New York. He worked on the Attica Railroad until he saved enough money to send for his family. When they arrived, Matthew rented a farm owned by Judge George Geddis. Judge Geddis had arrived in the area back in 1792. He owned an extensive amount of land and a salt manufacturing company.

Judge Geddis encouraged James Mulvaney to attend the local public school. The judge was a strong supporter of the public school system. He knew that James would have an advantage in making his way later in life if he had a good education. James attended school throughout his adolescent years.

When James was eighteen years old, he made his way to Michigan, arriving in Barry County. He found work as a farm laborer for the Ellis family in Assyria Township. After three years, James managed to save $160. He used the money to buy eighty acres of land from Mr. Ellis. James worked for Ellis and on his own farm in the spring and summer months. Due to the fact that he had received an education, he was able to supplement his earnings by teaching in the local school during the winter months.

In 1844, James returned to visit his family in Salina, New York. He encouraged his parents and siblings to return with him to his farm in Barry County. James explained that he had already built a house for all of them. All of the Mulvaneys made the journey to Michigan. Everyone worked to clear a large part of the 80 acres. Two years later, James's father offered to buy the land from him. James agreed, sold the land and made his way to Pennfield, in Calhoun County, Michigan. He hired himself out to William P. Smith, who owned a large farm and dairy. Once again, James saved his money in order to buy more land. This time, he purchased 133 acres in Pennfield Township, about twenty-five miles from the family farm. James married William Smith's daughter, Eliza, in 1848. Three years later, Eliza passed away, leaving James with three children.

James Mulvaney continued working and eventually purchased a second farm in Bellevue Township in Eaton County. James now owned 273 acres of land. He built two barns, a windmill and a large water tank. He planted two large orchards. He owned three teams of horses. He also owned two hundred sheep. He was the first farmer in Bellevue Township to breed full-blooded shorthorn cattle. His farms now served dual purposes—beef cattle and dairy products—which made James quite prosperous.

When the Grand Trunk Railroad Company proposed laying tracks through the county, James Mulvaney was one of the most ardent supporters. James wanted to see the railroad built, so he gave the rail company $400 to help finance the cost. James enjoyed seeing this idea come to fruition. He was heard to have said, with great satisfaction, "In the early days when I would take my ax and go to work, I could look out and see a train of deer, while now I look out upon a train of cars."

In 1857, James married a second time. His second wife was Eliza Paul. She and James had eight children together. They remained with their children in Pennfield Township. In his heart, James was simply a hardworking farmer who put his family first always. James Mulvaney died in 1912 at eighty-seven years of age.

BAY COUNTY

The Benefits of a Good Education

Women emigrating from Ireland did not have many lawful professions to choose from when they stepped off the boat. Many young girls went into service for the wealthy citizens of Boston and New York. Others found work in textile factories. Once a young woman married, her lot in life was to keep the family home intact and to raise the children. As immigrants settled into their new lives, some were able to obtain an education for their daughters as well as their sons. In many ways, it was the children and the grandchildren of immigrants who were able to take advantage of opportunities for advancing their standard of living.

Ellen Bean was the daughter of John and Ella White Bean. Her father, of County Kildare, Ireland, came to the United States while still a young man. Her mother, Ella, was born in County Tipperary in 1806. John arrived in New York and then found employment as a railroad contractor. After marrying, the two traveled to Toledo, Ohio. Ellen was born in Toledo on February 1, 1840, the second of eventually five children. She was five years old when the family moved to Adrian, Michigan. Her father again worked as a contractor on the railroad.

Ellen was fortunate in receiving a very good education. She attended and graduated from secondary school. At seventeen years of age, she began teaching in Medina Township in Lenawee County. Teaching in rural schools in the mid-1800s was no easy task. There could be up to sixty pupils in a one-room schoolhouse. The curriculum was basic: reading, writing, simple arithmetic, some geography and history. When older boys came to school, having a break from their farm work, they often flirted or teased the female teacher, who might be younger than themselves. School administrators who once frowned upon women teachers came to see that they were quite suited to the job. Additionally, women teachers were paid one-third the salary that male teachers received. It seemed to make good economic sense to hire women to teach the youngest students. It was thought that a woman's "natural femininity" was especially suited to teaching the very youngest children. Ellen eventually came to teach in the town of Adrian. She kept her teaching position until she accepted a proposal of marriage from John Kline, the principal of the Adrian schools. Married women were generally barred from keeping their posts as teachers. Her husband, John, was born in Pennsylvania in 1840. His family moved to White Pigeon in St. Joseph County, Michigan, when John was very young. John and Ellen were married on November 24, 1863.

John and Ellen Kline then moved with their family to Bay City, Michigan. John and a partner opened a grocery store, which was successful for the first four years. Unfortunately, one day it was destroyed by fire. The loss was too great to absorb financially. Later that same year, John passed away.

Ellen married again in January 1868. Her second husband was Thomas Deegan. He too had been born in County Tipperary, Ireland, in 1832. Thomas managed the Ontario Hotel in Bay City from 1865 until his death in 1874. Ellen remained in the family home with her children from both her first and second marriages. She owned real estate throughout Bay City. By virtue of her intelligence and education, she was considered to be an astute businesswoman. For a daughter of Irish immigrants, this was high praise indeed.

BENZIE COUNTY

Trees and the Lumber Trade, From the Ground Up

Lawrence W. Crane was born in County Wexford, Ireland, in 1837. At twelve years of age, he crossed the Atlantic with his parents, Martin and Anastasia Lee Crane. The family settled in Jefferson County, New York. The next year, Lawrence left home to travel to Chicago. There he was apprenticed to F. Scammon in his drugstore. He remained in Chicago for eighteen months.

In the latter months of 1851, Lawrence came to Michigan. He joined the thousands of other young men who found work in lumber camps and mills. Lumbering was a job for the wintertime, as sawing trees was much faster when the sap was not running. Hauling the newly cut logs over snow-covered ground was much more efficient than dragging them over rough trails. Many men worked on farms in the summertime and in the lumber camps in the wintertime. Lawrence successfully worked in many different aspects of the lumbering trade. Initially, he signed on at a lumber mill in Heron Creek, south of the town of Frankfort, in Benzie County. His job was that of the tail sawyer, working at the tail end of the carriage supporting logs for sawing. Lawrence kept at that job for eighteen months. His next job was in Muskegon, Michigan, marking and tallying lumber for a man named John Rudman. Following this job, he became the head sawyer in an Allegan County mill. The next spring, Lawrence switched jobs again when he took over the management of a mill in Saginaw, Michigan, owned by the Fisher & Lee Company. Eventually, Lawrence moved back to Muskegon, working as an engineer in the Pillsbury & Bradley Mill. Finally, Lawrence

Batteau crew. *Emerson Frank Greenman Papers, Bentley Historical Library, University of Michigan.*

took a job that placed him in charge of the Tyson and Robinson's gangmill in Manistee, Michigan. The gangmill was a machine that contained a heavy frame with multiple blades for cutting wood. Each position Lawrence held gained him more and better experience in the lumber industry. Lawrence remained with Tyson and Robinson until a fire destroyed the mill in 1868.

That same year, Lawrence accepted a position with a Detroit land company. He had married two years previously on November 21, 1866. He, his wife, Annette Rawlinson Crane, and their growing family moved to Frankfort, Michigan, so Lawrence could work directly for George S. Frost, one of the proprietors of the company. The company owned nearly all of the land around Frankfort. The town was located near a natural channel coming from the Aux Bec Scies River and leading into Lake Michigan. A survey had been carried out in 1864–65 to assess deepening the channel and enlarging the harbor at the lakeshore. George Frost employed Lawrence and other men to make improvements to the channel. Lawrence was instrumental in manufacturing the lumber for the harbor. Ships of any size would now be able to dock in Frankfort. Lawrence saw this as a great opportunity. A letter written and published in Frankfort in July 1867 expanded upon the settlement's potential:

> *The valuable hard timber surrounding this harbor, and extending back*
> *through the region of Benzonia, and beyond to the Manistee River, together*

with the valuable pine along the border of the Aux Becs Scies River, all covering a belt of the finest soil for agricultural purposes, the peculiar salubrity of the climate, its proximity to large bodies of water, and its many other natural advantages much render Frankfort in the future a place of much business and importance.

George Crane decided to go into business for himself, choosing to become a lumber dealer. He began to buy land on the Aux Bec Scies River, forming the Crane Lumber Company. Eventually, the company operated many lumber mills in the region. The principal mill was in Frankfort. Lawrence maintained his business for twenty-four years. The worth of the company climbed to $75,000 by the year 1884. The Crane Mill could cut forty thousand feet of lumber per day.

As a tree grows from the ground up, so Lawrence Crane learned the lumber trade.

BERRIEN COUNTY

A Plumber by Trade, A Patriot by Deed

Daniel Sheehan was born in the town of Portlaw, County Waterford, Ireland, on July 1, 1842. His parents were Cornelius Sheehan, a tailor, and Martha Pike. The Pike name was well known and respected in the cities of Cork and Waterford. Cornelius Sheehan immigrated to New York in the early 1840s. His wife and young son traveled to the port at Liverpool in order to follow him in 1844. The voyage for Daniel and his mother, made in rough and stormy weather, lasted for seven weeks and four days. The reunited family remained in New York for four years. Cornelius continued to work as a tailor during this time.

After four years in New York, the Sheehans decided to move to Assyria Township in Washtenaw County, Michigan. Cornelius's parents had already immigrated to Michigan along with four of their other children. They had established a home in Assyria and were eager for Cornelius and his family to join them. Daniel was six years old when he first came to Michigan. He attended the local public school. In his adolescence, Daniel learned the trade of plumbing. Six more children joined the growing Sheehan family.

In 1861, when the War Between the States broke out, Daniel was nineteen years old. He was eager to do his part and volunteered to join the Union army. Daniel traveled to Jackson, Michigan, where he enlisted in Company H, Michigan Twentieth Infantry, on August 19, 1862. The Twentieth Michigan was immediately deployed to Washington, D.C., where Confederate forces were driving back the Union forces and threatening the city. Only one month later, Daniel found himself east of Antietam Creek where the Union army finally halted the Confederate army's march. This was Daniel's first encounter on the battlefield. During that engagement, 3,700 men died.

From Antietam, Daniel's unit went on to engage in the Battles of the Wilderness in Northern Virginia, Spotsylvania, Cold Harbor, East Tennessee and the Siege of Vicksburg. In the Battle of Petersburg, Daniel was captured and taken prisoner. He managed to escape and returned to his company. Daniel was promoted to a full first sergeant in 1864 and became a full first lieutenant in May 1865. In July 1866, Daniel took part in the Grand Review in Washington, D.C.

Within the Twentieth Michigan Infantry regiment, Daniel Sheehan was one of only 21 men who survived the war. His regiment lost 13 officers and 111 enlisted men in battle; 3 officers and 175 men died of disease as a result of injuries sustained in battle.

After the war ended, Daniel returned to his family home. He once again took up work as a plumber. In 1867, Daniel married Mary "Minnie" Kearney in Ann Arbor, Michigan. Upon their marriage, they moved to Niles, Michigan, in Berrien County. Daniel found employment with John W. Payne, another plumber, in the city of Niles. When the leaders of the city came together to initiate a public waterworks system, Daniel bought inventory that included the necessary plumbing, gas and water fixtures. Later on, Daniel constructed the first sewer system in Niles. He later sold his ownership of the sewer system to the city, thus ensuring his prosperity.

Daniel was well respected in Niles, where he remained for the rest of his life. Minnie passed away in 1916, after forty-nine years of marriage, having given birth to six children. Daniel served as an alderman for the city of Niles. He built more than twenty houses, which he sold to other people eager to settle in Niles with their families. Daniel Sheehan, the patriot plumber, was eighty-two years old when he passed away in 1924.

BRANCH COUNTY

A Pair of Horses, A Covered Wagon, A Family Heads West

James Murphy grew up in Cayuga County, New York. He was born on March 4, 1819, to John and Rebecca Clay Murphy. John Murphy had emigrated from County Armagh in Ireland with his parents in 1810 when he was nine years old. His father, Patrick Murphy, bought land for their first homestead shortly after their arrival in New York. John continued to improve this homestead as he grew into adulthood, eventually bringing his wife, Rebecca, to live there as well. Their family grew to include ten children. Growing up, in addition to working on the family farm, their son James attended school. When he was twenty years old, in 1839, James married Mary Field. They remained on the family farm for three years.

In 1843, the James Murphy family decided to head for Michigan. James had heard that there was land aplenty there. The family traveled from Cayuga County, following the railroad as far as it ran west to Adrian, Michigan. They traveled in a covered wagon pulled by a pair of horses. Another family traveled with them. Both families had packed provisions for the journey and their cooking utensils so that they could prepare meals along the way. The journey took twenty-one days. The Murphys did not stop in Adrian. They continued on while they still had some money. In Batavia Township in Branch County, Michigan, James had only a five-franc piece still in his possession. The Murphys decided that here they would build a home.

James met a Mr. Parker, one of the original settlers of Batavia Township. Parker invited the Murphys to live with him while they searched for land to purchase. James chose a tract of seventy acres in Batavia Township, which he partially paid for by selling their pair of horses. James began building a log cabin, trading a carpet Mary had brought with them for boards to lay as a floor. The fireplace was built partly of stone and from dirt and sticks. James traded the bed they had for a yoke of oxen. With the oxen, he could begin clearing the land. It took James eight years to clear and make arable 60 acres. He gradually bought more land adjoining his own until the Murphy farm was 140 acres in size. Eventually, James bought even more land until he owned another 100 acres in a different section of the township.

Until 1850, no railroad had been laid farther than Hillsdale County, east of Branch County. From 1846 to 1850, the Southern Railroad Company had tried to raise the funds to continue building. In 1851, the railroad company was ready to build. During the summer months, track was laid in Branch County. The first locomotive chugged through the townships of Quincy, Coldwater, Batavia, Bethel and Bronson. The work continued all through the winter months, until, in March 1852, trains could travel west from Lake Erie all the way to Chicago. Three years later, another rail line was completed between Toledo, Ohio, and Buffalo, New York. Eventually, the railroad was extended to form a continuous connection from New York to Chicago, passing through Branch County.

Thousands of immigrants began to make their way west. Many new settlers came to Branch County. Between 1851 and 1861, the population increased from 12,472 to 20,981 residents. A centennial history of Branch County noted that during this time, previously vacant land was soon purchased for farms. The Murphy family and many other earlier settlers became prosperous, their homes and land improved and refined:

> In a majority of cases the log houses of the pioneers were exchanged for frames, pumps took the place of picturesque but inconvenient, well sweeps, which had formerly risen in every yard, orchards presented their luscious fruit in ample abundance, and school-houses and churches rose wherever necessary, to promote the intellectual and spiritual welfare of the people.

In forty years of life, James traveled over five hundred miles in a covered wagon, cleared land and built a home, married and raised a family, witnessed the railroad transform travel and the movement of goods and became a respected farming landowner.

CALHOUN COUNTY

Off to War—At Age Fourteen

John Whalen was born in Ireland on June 18, 1848. When he was only a few months old, his parents, John and Mary Malony Whalen, decided to immigrate to America. Upon their arrival, they made their way to Woonsocket Falls, in the state of Rhode Island. Woonsocket was just a small village, but John Whalen was able to hire himself out as a laborer and found steady employment. The family remained in Woonsocket for seven years and then moved to the town of Marshall in Calhoun County, Michigan.

Young John attended school while the family lived in Woonsocket. He was able to continue attending school until he turned thirteen years old. In 1861, John began working at various jobs wherever he could find them. The Civil War began, and in the spring of 1862, he volunteered to serve in the Union army. Although he was underage, he was sent with a company to St. Louis, Missouri. From St. Louis, the company was engaged in many battles across many states. John survived, but at the age of fourteen, he had already seen and experienced the horrifying devastation and death of war.

In January 1863, John left army service and returned to St. Louis. From St. Louis, he made his way to Detroit, where he reunited with his older brother William. William had been a tin peddler in Marshall. He would load a canvas sack with all sorts of useful pieces of tin spoons, pails and candle holders, as well as many other household necessities, and then he would set off walking. He walked between the settlements, visiting homesteads and showing his wares. A peddler provided goods to isolated communities where people lived far from towns. In Detroit, there were so

Presentation of colors, Campus Martius, Detroit, 1861. *Bentley Historical Library, University of Michigan.*

many people living in town, or coming into the town, that having his own shop was more profitable than peddling his wares. William took John on as a clerk in his hardware shop.

John's clerkship lasted until he found a different post. In 1865, the Metropolitan Police Department of Detroit was formed. The department was hiring men for a reorganized police force. John Whalen was one of the first men to be hired. Residential neighborhoods were expanding in size, and the newly hired policemen were collected by farm wagon at the beginning of their shift and then dropped off in various neighborhoods. The policemen walked through the neighborhood and business areas, keeping watch. At the end of their shifts, the wagon and driver returned to collect the patrolling officers. John stayed with the police force for three years before being promoted to sergeant. He served as a sergeant for five years but then resigned. He returned to Marshall because his father had passed away, leaving his mother on her own.

John opened a hardware store in Marshall. The town was growing quickly. There were nine churches, a large district union school and three other ward schools. John built up a successful trade. He enjoyed a good reputation among his customers. He was elected the city treasurer of Marshall in 1888, an office he held for a number of years. In 1890, when John was forty-two years old, he married Mary Henkel. Four years after their marriage, John passed away at the age of forty-six from Bright's Disease. He may not have remembered his birth country, but he served his new country starting from a very young age all through his life.

14

CASS COUNTY

Irish Roots, American Branches

Joseph Garrett was born and raised in Belfast, County Down, Ireland. He was not a man of means but did possess a warranty deed for ten acres of land. He farmed this land and raised his family here. Joseph married Ellen Orr. She gave birth to ten children, most of whom emigrated from Ireland in the first half of the nineteenth century. The oldest son was named Hugh, a shipbuilder by trade, who came to America soon after the nineteenth century began. Hugh settled in Cincinnati, Ohio. A few years later, Hugh's brother John left the family home as well. John made the voyage across the Atlantic in 1818 at nineteen years old. The voyage lasted three months. During part of this time, the ship met an iceberg and was unable to move for many days. Eventually, John and the other passengers landed in New York.

From New York, John made his way to Philadelphia, Pennsylvania. From Philadelphia, he walked west to Cincinnati, a distance of five hundred miles. In Cincinnati, John was reunited with Hugh. John did not have much money. He learned the skills needed to become a cooper. Later, he found work in a distillery. Ten years after his arrival in Cincinnati, John married Rosa Petticrew. Rosa was born in Montgomery County, Ohio, in 1808. John and Rosa moved to Montgomery County, where Rosa owned forty acres of land. John bought a farm of one hundred acres, which he added to Rosa's land. They lived on the farm for the next eighteen years. Their first son, named Hugh Patrick Garrett, was born on October 26, 1830. Following Hugh Patrick, nine more children were born into the family.

In 1848, John sold his farm. The family moved to Cass County, Michigan. Rosa's uncle, John Petticrew, had settled in Cass County in 1830. He was the first to erect a sawmill in Jefferson Township. All of the equipment for the mill had to be carted from Ohio in a wagon pulled by a team of oxen. John was not interested in buying land in Cass County. Instead, he purchased eighty acres of farmland in neighboring Van Buren County. This was his home until 1862, when he passed away at the age of sixty-three years.

Hugh Patrick was eighteen years old when the family came to Cass County. He liked the look of the land in LaGrange Township and hired himself out by the month for farm work so that he could save enough money to buy his own farm. In 1854, when he was twenty-four years old, Hugh Patrick and Elizabeth White married. Within only a few years, Elizabeth died. A few years later, Hugh Patrick married a second time. His second wife, Julia, was the daughter of Samuel and Catherine Dunn. Julia was born in Franklin County, Indiana. She too had been widowed and was already the mother of two children when she married Hugh Patrick. For a few years, Julia and Hugh Patrick lived in Franklin County where they farmed. Two children were born to them. The family moved back to Cass County when Hugh Patrick purchased one hundred acres of land in 1865. Forty-six acres were ready for cultivation. Hugh Patrick set about clearing and improving the rest of the acreage. Nine years later, he was widowed again when Julia passed away at the age of forty-four in 1874. Hugh Patrick married a third time; he and Phoebe Struble married on October 26, 1876, in Niles, Michigan. Phoebe had one daughter from a previous marriage. She and Hugh Patrick had three more children. Their daughter, Rosa, named for Hugh Patrick's mother, died at the age of eighteen in 1903. Three weeks later, Phoebe died as well. Through all of his years, Hugh Patrick Garrett continued to improve his farm, aided by his sons. The Irish roots of Hugh Patrick's family tree had grown into strong branches on American soil.

15

CHARLEVOIX COUNTY

The Other Emerald Isle

In northeastern Lake Michigan, there is an archipelago of islands. French explorers in the 1600s named the largest island Beaver Island for its large beaver population. French fur traders and Irish fishermen arrived in the early 1800s. They found Beaver Island inhabited by indigenous people. Fish and beaver pelts were so plentiful that Beaver Island became an important port for traders and merchants.

In 1847, James Strang arrived on Beaver Island. He was the leader of a group following the Mormon religion. Strang decided Beaver Island would be the congregation's new home. His charisma and rhetoric soon brought many more followers to the island. By 1850, his followers outnumbered the non-Mormon residents. Strang proclaimed that all persons living on Beaver Island must convert to Mormonism or leave. He arrived at each house, accompanied by armed followers. Even the lighthouse keeper and his family had to leave. Most of the Irish islanders went to Mackinac Island or Gull Island to salvage their fishing livelihoods.

On July 8, 1850, Strang proclaimed himself a temporal king. He commanded his followers to obey orders that were not agreeable to them. Discontent simmered until one day, Strang was shot by two of his followers. He was taken to Wisconsin, where he died. News of Strang's departure spread quickly. The Irish fishermen hastened to return, and Strang's followers were routed from the island.

When the Irish islanders wrote home to Ireland, they said that Beaver Island reminded them of Ireland. They encouraged their relatives to come join them in a new Emerald Isle. Letters reached the Irish community on the island of

Aran Mor, off the coast of County Donegal. The entire island had been ruined by the potato famine years. Most of the community decided to immigrate to Beaver Island. They made their way to Canada and across to Michigan, then boarded a boat to Beaver Island. So many Irish arrived, over 95 per cent of the islanders were first- or second-generation Irish. Beaver Island was a Gaeltacht, a place where the Irish language was the dominant language.

Father Peter Gallagher, an emigrant from County Mayo, was assigned to serve the mostly Catholic population on the island. He arrived on Beaver Island in 1865 and was a fluent Gaelic speaker and man of the people. Island residents who passed their remembrances on to their descendants and historians remembered Father Gallagher in this way: "He settled disputes, loaned money, arranged marriages, carried on with the bachelors, acquired vast holdings, owned the merchant ship Hattie Fisher, and became an avid hunter and fisherman." However, Father Gallagher had not completed his training for the priesthood. He was sent to Beaver Island after only two years of study. He knew how to conduct a Mass but did not know much about theology or sacramental instruction. It was the custom that the bishop would visit remote places where incompletely trained priests were assigned to give them an examination. The bishop decided then whether the priest was fit for his spiritual duty.

Father Gallagher and his parishioners learned of the bishop's impending visit, and everyone knew that Father Gallagher must not be given an examination. When the bishop arrived, he was escorted off the boat. Some men quickly accosted the boat captain, telling him that if he did not leave immediately with the bishop on board, he might not be leaving at all. The captain took the islanders at their word. He hailed the bishop and told him that they must leave. The bishop had not even seen Father Gallagher, but the captain was insistent. The bishop reboarded the boat.

Father Gallagher "gave out" at times to parishioners who were not practicing the faith. One day, inside the church, he confronted a man about missing Mass. The men began arguing and then exchanged punches with each other. The bishop heard about Father Gallagher fighting inside the church and deconsecrated the building so no more services could be held there. Father Gallagher was transferred off the island.

Beaver Island was once the largest supplier of freshwater fish in the United States. Eventually, by 1886, overfishing had ruined the industry. Lumbering became the next industry. The Beaver Island Lumber Company started operations in 1901 and remained in business until all of the usable trees were cut down. The Irish influence remained strong. Saint Patrick's Day was celebrated with Irish music and dancing and storytelling. Their ways were known as the "island way." Beaver Island was for them the "other" Emerald Isle.

16

CHEBOYGAN COUNTY

A Long Way from Tipperary

James Maloney was born in County Tipperary, Ireland, in 1841 to James L. Maloney and Ellen O'Neill Maloney. In 1857, the family, which also included a son named Patrick, born in 1852, left Ireland for the United States. They settled in the state of New York. James was sixteen years old, and almost immediately after the ship docked, he began looking for work. He found intermittent employment as a laborer. James kept on working for ten years. During that time, he saved as much money as he was able. James had in mind to move to the growing city of Detroit. Gathering his savings and whatever else he could carry, James traveled to Detroit, where he started up a grocery business. Three years later, James married Bridget Brown, another Irish immigrant. They remained in Detroit until 1876. That year, James and Bridget, along with their three children, moved to the village of Cheboygan in Cheboygan County, Michigan. One year later, their fourth child was born.

As he had done in Detroit, James opened a grocery store. A few years later, his brother Patrick joined him. It was a smart business move opening the grocery because Cheboygan County was beginning to experience an upsurge in population growth. From 1870 through 1880, the county census showed that the resident population had tripled. The Maloneys had arrived in the midst of the booming lumber industry. James and Patrick opened two more grocery stores along the Lake Huron shore. They also bought into a bottling works company located in the village of Au Sable.

With keen perception, James and Patrick realized that while their grocery businesses were doing well, what lumbermen really wanted was beer. Most of the lumberjacks were young, single men. After their week's work in the lumber camps, forests, sawmills and along the river, men were ready to relax on their one day in town. They ceased operating the grocery stores to start a brewery, opening the Northern Brewery in 1883. The opening was headline news in the local newspaper, the *Cheboygan Democrat*.

The beer was an immediate success. The Northern Brewery began producing forty barrels of beer a day. The brothers engaged two boats to convey their products to towns along the shoreline of northern Michigan. In 1890, the name of the business became the Cheboygan Brewing and Malting Company. James bought out Patrick's share of the company. Patrick had married a few years earlier and now had his own family. Patrick started his own bottling business. His brother James was his most valued customer.

By 1909, two of Cheboygan Brewing's brands—the Silvio and the Bohemian—became the most popular beers around the saloons of northern Michigan. They were advertised as "Two grand beverages for people who appreciate a mild stimulant that is at the same time nutritious and beautiful." The brewing company and its famous beers were a great success while lumbering was the primary occupation in Cheboygan County. Eventually, though, the trees were all cut down. Lumber camps closed, and sawmills no longer had enough work to keep them open. By the beginning of the second decade of the twentieth century, lumbering was no longer big business in Cheboygan County. At the same time, the temperance movement had reached northern Michigan. The Cheboygan Brewing Company closed its doors in 1911. James Maloney, while no longer a brewer, was a very wealthy man. He became the president of a local bank in Cheboygan. Until the end of his days, James enjoyed his prosperity a long way from Tipperary.

17

CHIPPEWA COUNTY

First Native American Woman of Literature

Jane Johnston Schoolcraft was born in Sault Ste. Marie on January 31, 1800. She was the daughter of John Johnston from Belfast, Ireland, and Ozhaguscodawayquay, or Susan Johnston, the daughter of the Ojibwe chief Waubojeeg. Jane was one of eight children. Her father and mother were active in the fur trade, building a trading post in Sault Ste. Marie that prospered. They were respected in the community of traders, trappers and Ojibwe people.

John Johnston was born in 1762 in Belfast. His father was a civil engineer who designed the Belfast Waterworks. His maternal uncle was the attorney general of Ireland. John owned an estate near the town of Coleraine in County Londonderry. As a young man, he became interested in the fur trade going on in Canada. In 1790, he sailed to Montreal. After arriving, he introduced himself to the owners of the Northwest Company of Montreal, dealers in furs. John left Montreal for Sault Ste. Marie, Michigan, where he took up trading at the frontier post located there.

Chief Waubojeeg was chief of the north shore of Lake Huron and both shores of Lake Superior. He came to know John Johnston at the trading post and learned that John wished to marry Ozhaguscodawayquay. Ozhaguscodawayquay, "Woman of the Green Valley," was said to be "the surest eye and fleetest foot among the women of the tribe." The chief rebuffed John's request to marry Ozhaguscodawayquay, but John was persistent. Chief Waubojeeg told him, "White Man, I have noticed your

Jane Johnston Schoolcraft. *Bentley Historical Library, University of Michigan.*

behavior, it has been correct; Of you, may I expect better things. You say you are going to Montreal; go, and if you return I shall be satisfied of your sincerity and will give you my daughter." John did return. He and Ozhaguscodawayquay married, and she took the name Susan Johnston. Their first daughter was Bamewawagezhikaquay, Jane Johnston. Her name meant, "The sound the stars make rushing through the sky."

Jane's mother taught her the Ojibwe language and stories, as well as needlework and household duties. John taught Jane English, reading, writing and speaking. She studied the Bible and read from her father's extensive library. In 1809, Jane and her father traveled to Ireland. John had business to conduct regarding his estate. Jane stayed with her relatives, John and Jane Johnston Moore, in County Wexford. She continued her education in Ireland. Later, Jane and her father traveled to England.

In 1820, Governor Lewis Cass traveled to Sault Ste. Marie accompanied by soldiers. He wanted to establish a military presence in the area. The local people did not want this. Ozhaguscodawayquay used her influence to persuade the tribe to cede land for a fort. Henry Rowe Schoolcraft was traveling with Governor Cass. He was interested in Ojibwe culture, language and history. Schoolcraft was appointed the agent for Indian affairs in Michigan, with his office in Sault Ste. Marie.

In 1823, Henry and Jane married. Jane, her mother and her siblings taught Henry the Ojibwe language and about traditions and the culture of the tribe. Henry wrote down the stories of the Ojibwe people, aided by Jane, who was of immense help to him in this endeavor. Both Henry and Jane were well known in the community of Sault Ste. Marie.

Jane gave birth to Panaysee, "Little Bird," in 1824. His English name was William Henry. She gave birth the following year to a stillborn daughter. Panaysee lived only three years, which greatly saddened Jane. Later, two more children were born who grew to adulthood.

In 1826, Henry and Jane produced a literary magazine about the Ojibwe people called *The Literary Voyager*, or *Muzzenyegun*. Fourteen issues were published and widely read. The issues contained original stories that Jane penned using pseudonyms and some retellings of traditional Ojibwe stories. Jane was not given written credit by Henry for her contributions.

Jane became a voice for the Ojibwe people, recording and sharing their traditional stories. The stories portrayed Ojibwe values of "truth, rationality, logic and causality" as well as the Ojibwe way of knowing. Her work saved Ojibwe stories from extinction. One theme in Ojibwe stories that Jane revisited many times was the importance of family. Two of her retellings, "Mishosha, or the Magician and his Daughters" and "The Forsaken Brother," illustrate this theme.

Jane's health was never robust after the birth of her children. She was often sickly. Her marriage to Henry was not, after all, a happy one, and she went to live with her sister in Dundas, Ontario. She died suddenly on May 22, 1842, when she was forty-two years old.

Jane's collection of stories inspired the poet Henry Wadsworth Longfellow. He borrowed from them to compose his epic poem *The Song of Hiawatha*, published in 1855. Jane's legacy earned her the title "First Native American Woman of Literature."

18

CLARE COUNTY

He Wore Many Hats

Michael Quinn was born in Ireland in 1798. He and his wife, Ann, were the parents of eight children. During the potato famine years, four of their children died from starvation. Desperate to escape further tragedy, the Quinn family immigrated to America, arriving in New York in 1849. Michael was able to buy land for a farm in Seneca, New York. A son John was born in Seneca on November 15, 1854.

The family remained in Seneca for fifteen years, until 1864, when they moved to Calhoun County, Michigan. John's brothers, Michael, Joseph and Peter, enlisted in the Union army during the Civil War. Michael died from the wounds he received during the war. Joseph, a member of the U.S. Navy, survived the war, but he later drowned in Saginaw, Michigan. Peter, who was sixteen when he enlisted, also survived the war. The Quinns lived in Calhoun County for eighteen years. John attended public school in Battle Creek, Michigan.

When John was twenty years old, he headed for Saginaw, where he found employment in a shingle mill. The work involved slicing logs into thin shingles for roofing. Twice, John was involved in accidents with the shingle slicer, resulting in the loss of fingers on both hands. The injuries forced John to return to the family home, where he decided to continue his education.

Eventually, John was hired to work as a bookkeeper for the W.H. & F.A. Wilson Lumber Company. The company was located in Isabella County, Michigan. The Wilson family owned nearly two thousand acres of forest land in Clare and Isabella Counties. Lumbering was king in Michigan.

Lumber mill, Clare County. *Michigan State University Archives and Historical Collections.*

The population of once small outposts was exploding. Isabella County experienced a threefold increase in population from four thousand to twelve thousand people in the ten years between 1870 and 1880. Clare County experienced a tenfold increase from nearly four hundred to four thousand people during the same time. John worked for the Wilson Company for twelve years.

In 1878, John Quinn and Jennie Dodge married. The couple had two sons, William and Stanley. They moved to the town of Harrison in Clare County, where John started a local newspaper, the *Clare County Cleaver*. His partner was John Canfield, a local butcher. The first edition of the newspaper was printed in the back room of Canfield's shop, leading to the newspaper's name. After eight years, John sold his portion of the business in order to accept a new position.

John was appointed postmaster by the postmaster general of the United States in 1889, and Jennie served as the clerk. John was required to live in the town where the post office was located as well as post a bond. He could carry on with other businesses, but the post office had to be open during regular business hours. As postmaster, John was exempt from military service, but he could be called on to maintain the post roads. During his four-year tenure, John had a share in a hardware shop known as Stephen and Quinn. He also owned a sawmill and then a livery service. He was the proprietor of the Johnson House, a local hotel. He even studied and read law and then was admitted to the bar in November 1893. One year later, John was elected prosecuting attorney for Clare County.

Harrison, Michigan, in the 1890s, was a town of two thousand residents. Thousands of lumberjacks came into town weekly, swelling the population. There were twenty-two saloons, a dozen restaurants and five hotels. Harrison took on the moniker of the "Toughest Town in Michigan." Lawlessness was rampant. John Quinn took on those who helped to create that reputation. He wore many different hats during his lifetime and wore them all well.

19

CLINTON COUNTY

In the News

John W. Fitzgerald was born in Rochester, New York, on March 16, 1845. His father, Michael, was an emigrant from Ireland. His mother, Mary McMahon, was born in Canada. When John was eight years old, his parents decided to relocate in Michigan. John attended school and graduated from high school. When he was eighteen years old, he became a soldier in the Union army. He enlisted as a private in Company G, the Third Michigan Cavalry Regiment. John saw action in battles fought in the Southern states. After the war ended, he traveled back to Michigan.

John decided to take up journalism upon his return to civilian life. He became the owner, editor and publisher of the *Ovid Register*, the newspaper of the village of Ovid, in Clinton County. He continued the newspaper for two and a half years. He also married Gertrude Yerkes, from Northville, Michigan, on October 7, 1868. John and Gertrude had two children, a daughter and a son.

In rural villages, most newspapers were a one-man show in the mid-1800s. Newspapers had already come a long way, evolving from handwritten pages painstakingly recopied a number of times. While a printing press allowed multiple productions of a newspaper, the press still had to be set letter by letter. East Coast cities were the recipients of multiple newspapers after the War for Independence, but the cost of a newspaper was prohibitive for many. In 1830, when the first penny newspaper was printed, the distribution of news became available to a much wider audience. Even newly arrived immigrants could find a penny for a newspaper. Those who could read learned about opportunities for work. Those who could not read found someone to read the newspaper for them.

As immigrants and other pioneers moved westward, printing presses went along, hauled on wagons or floated on barges. With the invention of the Linotype, a printer's work became much easier. As each letter did not have to be set individually, an entire line of words could be accomplished at one time. Political parties often had their own newspapers, and the editor was often the head of a political party. In this way, a party could showcase its candidates and their causes.

Unlike big city newspapers, rural newspapers came and went, usually determined by the editor-publisher-printer. Over the next few years, John Fitzgerald started up a number of newspapers. In 1872, he published the *Chesaning Times*. He took a few years off in order to work for the postal service but then partnered with James S. DeLand to publish the *Jackson Evening Times*, followed by the *Clinton and Shiawassee Union* newspaper. John served as the editor of this newspaper until 1886. He and Gertrude lived in Ovid and were now the parents of four children.

As a newspaperman, John was known to be well informed about people and events locally and nationally. He received the Republican Party nomination for the office of the Clinton County register of deeds for the 1886 election. He won the election and began a two-year term of office. When his first term ended, he was reelected and served another two-year term. He also served on the local school board over the next nine years. When the Business Men's Association of St. Johns was inaugurated, John served as the first president.

In 1891, John's career took another turn. He accepted a position with the State Bank of St. Johns as a cashier and worked for the bank for many years. His three sons all entered the journalism field. His oldest son became the editor and owner of the *Flint Journal* newspaper. His two younger sons became reporters for the *Los Angeles Times*. Gertrude passed away in 1898 at the age of fifty-two. John remarried in 1900. His second wife was Lena Baird. John was not quite done with holding political office, as he was elected mayor of St. Johns. Once again, his integrity and amiability inspired trust among the residents of the town. Lena and John lived many years together after John retired from the bank. John passed away at the age of eighty-six on September 19, 1931. The account of his life was worthy of being in the news.

20

CRAWFORD COUNTY

Finding His Niche

George Mahon was born in Ireland in 1848 to John and Hannah Ingram Mahon. George was born during one of the worst years of the Great Famine. At the age of fourteen, George immigrated by himself to Canada, settling in the city of Quebec. When George was twenty-five years old, he decided to move to Michigan.

George settled in St. Louis, Michigan, in 1872. During this time, he married Nettie Bagley, and they began to raise a family. The Mahon family moved north from St. Louis to Grayling, Michigan, in Crawford County in 1904. The town of Grayling had a population of under three thousand. Fishing and lumbering were the two prevalent occupations, but George did not take up either. Instead, he worked as a tailor. He also studied law in Ann Arbor. His immigrant status, working-class background and little formal education did not deter him. At the end of his studies, however, he was not admitted to the bar. George returned to Grayling with legal specializations in criminal law, real estate and commercial civil law.

Even without a lawyer's shingle, George was elected justice of the peace for Crawford County. He retained this position for the rest of his life, which amounted to three terms. He also worked as a collector for the Northern Michigan Agency, an insurance provider. George also worked as a fee collector for real estate owners in and around Grayling. He was also a notary public. George served the public in noncontentious matters concerning estates, deeds and wills. He was often called on to act as a witness when important documents were signed. George Mahon became very active in the local Republican Party and took his citizenship duties very seriously.

Nettie Mahon passed away in 1909. George had four young children living at home with him. He was fortunate in that he had many friends throughout his years in Grayling. He was kept busy with his official duties. Eventually, though, the children grew up. His son, George, moved to Detroit. The other children looked in on their father when they could. George began taking his meals in the same restaurant every evening.

It was the predictability of George's routine that put his friends wise to the fact that something was wrong with him. After taking a meal in his usual restaurant on a Sunday, George was not seen again. George's friends began to wonder about his whereabouts. After two more days, a group of friends went to George's house. The doors were locked, but with feelings of desperation, the group decided that it would be best to break into the house. They managed to get a door opened. Inside, they found George. He was sitting up in his sitting room, dressed in his night robe, dead.

A police investigation followed. The official report stated that death had occurred in the night. The cause of death was listed as apoplexy, or stroke. George was seventy-two years old. A dignified man who worked diligently and lived quietly slipped away in the night after finding his niche in Crawford County.

21

DELTA COUNTY

The Pioneer Pharmacist

Henry Coburn was born in Clinton County, Michigan, on March 23, 1848. Henry's parents, Lewis and Lucinda Hayes Coburn, were born in the state of New York to Irish and Scots immigrants. Lewis was born in 1806 and Lucinda in 1813. Lewis and Lucinda lived for a time in the state of Vermont, but in 1838, they decided to move to Michigan. They settled in DeWitt Township in Clinton County and cleared land for a farm. Lewis was both a local Methodist clergyman and a circuit riding preacher. Five children came into the family. Henry was the fourth child born. He attended public school in Clinton County and then began going to school in Lansing when he was twelve years old. After a few years, Henry was also able to attend the newly established Agricultural College of the State of Michigan. The college had opened its doors in 1857 as the first agricultural college in the United States. In its initial years, the college consisted of three buildings, five faculty members and sixty-three male students. The first president, Joseph R. Williams, was a strong proponent of higher education for young men from farming and working-class backgrounds. Henry studied at the agricultural college for four years. He, like many of the other students, was required to perform three hours of daily manual labor, which helped to keep costs down both for the students and for the college.

In 1870, at the age of twenty-two, Henry Coburn relocated to Detroit. Detroit was a bustling metropolis, with immigrants streaming into the city—some to remain, and many to continue their movement north or westward. Henry decided to study pharmacy while he was in Detroit.

There was not much governmental regulation of medicinal products, but Henry had received a sound background in the sciences, which stood him well during his training. William Proctor, the "Father of American Pharmacy," had argued back in 1844 that a basic science education should be a requisite for the purpose of pursuing a pharmacy course.

Henry completed his studies in Detroit and then moved to Marquette, Michigan, in 1877. Great strides and innovations were occurring in the field of pharmacology, and mechanization led to mass production of known medicines. Progress in transportation led to faster and more efficient delivery of medicine. In 1885, innovations such as the medicinal tablet, coated pills and gelatin capsules were produced by the Parke, Davis and Company of Detroit. This company became the oldest and largest drug company in America. Parke, Davis and Company built the first modern pharmaceutical laboratory. It developed methods for performing clinical trials of new medicines. Men like Henry, who had been trained to mix and construct medicines on their own, saw their skills being replaced by mechanization in the pharmacological industry.

Henry remained in Marquette for the next ten years. While in Marquette, in 1885, he and Catherine Schaffer married. Two years later, Henry and Catherine moved to Schaffer Township in Delta County, Michigan. They lived here for thirteen years while Henry was involved in a mercantile business. Eventually, in 1900, they moved to Escanaba, Michigan. Henry returned to working as a druggist. He was appointed postmaster in Escanaba in 1906. Henry was still mixing and dispensing medicines even after his seventieth birthday. He was a true pioneer in many aspects of his life: as a young man from a rural background who was able to obtain a college education, in the choice of his life's work as a druggist in the early days of pharmacological training and in the place where he settled, the northern peninsula of Michigan in the latter years of the nineteenth century.

22

DICKINSON COUNTY

Making Our Father Proud

Patrick O'Callaghan of County Clare, Ireland, was born on March 16, 1816. His father was another Patrick O'Callaghan, and his mother was Mary Corbitt. Young Patrick traveled by himself to Canada in 1837. After landing in Quebec, he made his way to Buckingham Township. He became one of the thousands of men working in a lumber camp. Within a few years, Patrick purchased farm property, and he married Mary Cox in 1842. They raised five sons and two daughters while working on their farm.

The oldest son was John O'Callaghan, born in 1844. When John was twenty-five, he set out for Michigan's Upper Peninsula with his younger brother George, who was twenty-one. The brothers settled in Escanaba, a booming lumbering town. Lumber from Escanaba was sent throughout the Midwest for shipbuilding as well as for constructing houses and businesses.

The brothers found work as lumbermen. They worked hard, saved their money and eventually purchased a lumber company. John married in 1871, but his wife and two of their three children succumbed to tuberculosis. After the tragedies, their father left Canada to join them. Their brother James also relocated to Escanaba. He worked as a clerk in the company store for six months. He then enrolled in a commercial course at the Oshkosh Business College in Wisconsin. The lumber company was successful, but in 1877, John decided they should sell the business and move north to Norway Township in Dickinson County.

During the next year, the first iron mine, the Norway Mine, was established near the township. When the brothers reached Norway, they built a sawmill.

They knew that the mining company would require a great deal of lumber for operations, and the business grew quickly. When James finished his business course, he rejoined his brothers. He bought an interest in the sawmill and became the bookkeeper and then the manager. The sawmill was known as O'Callaghan Brothers and Company. John became the first supervisor of Norway Township. As the only taxpayer, he was the only man eligible to vote in the initial township meetings. John cast the sole vote to approve raising money for building Norway's first school.

On May 25, 1881, a spark ignited sawdust in the mill. Moments later, the spark gained momentum, causing a fire that grew too quickly to extinguish. When the fire was finally out, the mill was a total loss. The O'Callaghans went right to work rebuilding it, enlarging the site as they went along. Three months later, the new mill was up and running. The sign at the entrance read, "O'Callaghan Brothers: Manufacturers of rough and dressed lumber. Shingles, Cedar Posts, ties, car sills, bridge timbers, doors, sash, blinds, etc."

With George and James running the Norway mill, John decided to marry again. He and his second wife, Mary McLean, moved to Sagola, where John opened another lumbering company. He and Mary became parents to eleven children. Tuberculosis again struck John's family. Mary passed away from the disease in 1901, leaving John with eight children. With his own health in decline, John sold the mill in Sagola and returned to Norway. His father passed away in 1903. The newspaper account of Patrick O'Callaghan's passing praised him as "a pioneer and one whose rugged and genial personality will long be remembered."

George married Mary Ann Woods in 1883. James married Mary McGeehan in 1886. Many children were born into each family, but few survived diseases, injuries and acute infections. Both George and James strove to build and improve their town. George built a large block of stores at the foot of Main Street and then found business tenants for all of them. He built an opera house on the site of the former O'Callaghan family home. George built the first cement sidewalk in front of the new block of buildings. James took an active civic role in the town. He was elected to the board of education and served for three years. He promoted the organization of a savings and loan association and served as one of its first directors. James also served as the mayor of Norway for one term.

The O'Callaghan sons made their father proud through their hard work and in their loyalty to each other.

23

EATON COUNTY

A Cattle-Driving Man

David Nelson, his wife, Jane, and their two daughters sailed to the United States in 1824 or 1825. David was born in 1791 in the village of Killinchy, overlooking Strangford Lough in County Down, Ireland. Jane was born in 1799 in the nearby village of Kilmood. The family settled in Wayne County, Michigan, after their arrival. A son, David, was born in 1836.

The family farm was in Congress Township. David remained at home until he reached nineteen years of age. He had already saved enough money to purchase his own farm, so he traveled northwest to Eaton County. In Bellevue Township, David bought forty acres of land at $1.50 per acre. He planned to clear the land for farming. David lived in Bellevue Township but then sold his property in order to purchase more acres in Assyria Township in Barry County. He cleared this land, then planted grain and bought livestock. A few years later, David sold this property.

In 1865, David returned to Bellevue Township, where he bought eighty acres of farmland. Over the years, he built a house, barns, a windmill, a water tank, granaries and sheds. During harvest time, David engaged in threshing for other farmers. He became well known to all of the other farmers in the area. David and Murcie Wood, a farmer's daughter, decided to marry. Their family farm came to include their eight children.

By 1870, David had real estate valued at $3,200. His personal estate was valued at $700. He became involved in stock buying, as well as stock driving in and around Bellevue. Before the construction of the Grand Trunk Railroad in Eaton County in 1886, cattle driving was the method for moving cattle from place to place. David Nelson's cattle drives began in Bellevue, and from there, he drove cattle through Marshall, Battle Creek and Nashville, Michigan, and on to Chicago, nearly two hundred miles away. Sometimes, David took the cattle in the opposite direction to Buffalo, New York, over three hundred miles from Bellevue. A single long drive usually required ten drivers as well as periods of rest for both the men and the cattle. The cattle were driven for relatively short distances, allowing for rest periods at midday and at night. This gave the animals time to graze and recover before the next day. A balance between the desire to get the cattle to market as quickly as possible and the need to maintain the animals at the current marketable weight was a daily concern. On average, a herd could maintain a healthy weight moving at fifteen miles per day. It took David two weeks to drive cattle from Bellevue to Chicago or twenty days for the drive to Buffalo.

David managed to keep up his own farm even while away on the cattle drives. He was a civic-minded man who served as the Bellevue Township Supervisor for many years. He was chairman of the county board for one year as well. He believed in contributing to the development of his community.

In the winter of 1889, influenza swept through Russia and spread rapidly throughout Europe. The flu then spread to North America, ferried by passengers crossing the ocean. In the United States, the virus was transported by the ever-increasing number of people traveling on trains. This was the first modern pandemic that was recorded in detailed records. Over one million people died. David Nelson was a victim of the influenza. He passed away on July 6, 1890. The cattle-driving man had completed his last drive.

24

EMMET COUNTY

When Opportunity Knocks

John Quinlan was born in County Tipperary, Ireland, in 1817. He immigrated to New York before he was twenty years old. From New York, he traveled to the town of Charlotte in Chittenden County, Vermont. He found employment on the farm of Judge Edgar Meech, who owned 3,500 acres of land. John supplemented his income by selling cords of wood, priced at fifteen cents per cord. Lumber was plentiful in the region, so it was not long before John had saved enough money to buy his own farm in Charlotte.

In April 1838, John and Elizabeth Flood, also an Irish immigrant, married. They had five sons; the youngest was Thomas, born in 1848. Thomas grew up on the family farm and attended the local school built on his father's property. While the children were growing up, John Quinlan expanded his business interests. He became a buyer and seller of livestock. His sons participated in cattle drives, taking cattle to markets oftentimes one hundred miles from home. By 1870, John Quinlan had a personal estate valued at $5,000 and real estate worth $40,000. The patriarch of the family lived to be eighty-one years of age. He passed away in 1899.

When Thomas Quinlan was fourteen years old, he walked each day to the town of Ferrisburg, where he worked as a clerk in a general store. Thomas knew that he would not inherit the family farm, as that would go to the oldest son. Five years later, he found work as a clerk in the McWilliams Brothers firm in Burlington, Vermont. Thomas did not stay with the firm because ill health forced him to return home. When he recovered, he worked for his father again for another two years.

In October 1871, Thomas was twenty-three years old. Fred Meech, son of the judge, offered Thomas a business opportunity. Meech needed someone to manage his business in the town of Norwood, in Charlevoix County, Michigan. Thomas accepted the offer. He moved to Michigan, living and working in Norwood for three years. After this, Thomas wanted to go into business for himself. He became a wholesale buyer of potatoes, which he sold in the Chicago markets. He began to make contacts among the other merchants and farmers around the towns of Charlevoix and Torch Lake, as well as Norwood. He became acquainted with the firm of Fox, Rose and Butters, based in Charlevoix. In November 1874, Thomas was put in charge of the firm's store in Petoskey, Michigan, in neighboring Emmet County.

Thomas arrived in Petoskey at the same time as train service from Chicago began. The population of the town grew rapidly. Men found work in limestone mining and lumbering. The lumber was shipped south on Lake Michigan, with much of it going to Chicago to rebuild the city after the Great Chicago Fire of 1871. Thomas worked for Fox, Rose and Butters until 1878. He then went into partnership with a man named Philip Wachtel. Together, they established the first bank in Petoskey. The following year, Thomas and Philip's sister, Mary Barbara, were married.

As a bank manager, Thomas became aware of the great need for houses and land as more settlers came into the region. Thomas sold his share of the bank to W.L. Curtis of Kalamazoo in order to open a real estate and mortgage insurance business. Three of his sons joined him. Their firm was known as the Thomas Quinlan and Sons Company. Thomas's dealings with farmers over the years provided him with good insights, which he shared with new settlers. Thomas owned six hundred acres of land. He bred cattle and hogs and Shropshire sheep. He became the registrar of deeds for two terms in Emmet County, followed by serving as the township treasurer for Petoskey. Throughout his life, Thomas answered the door when opportunity knocked, making the most of his opportunities through hard work and determination. He passed away at the age of sixty-seven in 1915.

25

GENESEE COUNTY

Forging a New Life

O n December 13, 1834, John Eagan was born in County Longford, Ireland, to Michael and Mary Murtagh Eagan. Michael was a thatcher by trade as well as a mechanic. All over Ireland, houses had roofs made of thatch. Some could afford slates for their roofing, but the vast majority of people relied on local materials for their homes. Rushes and straw from wheat, flax, oats and rye were used as thatching material. A sod base was laid down first, and then bundles of straw fibers were woven through lengths of other fibers to form a watertight mesh to roof the house. Thatching was physically hard work undertaken all year round. The thatched roof was usually replaced annually. A thatcher did not earn much for his long hours, in spite of the essential necessity of his work. As a thatcher's son, John Eagan did not have a future ahead of him. He attended school whenever his father did not require his assistance on the family farm or at a thatching job. School was a "hedge" school, where students met in someone's house, or in a field, or beneath a hedgerow. Children basically learned to read and write. Most children attended school for a few months in the wintertime after the harvest season ended.

When John was fifteen years old, his father passed away. John's future prospects looked bleak, so he decided to immigrate to America. His mother traveled with him. They made their way to Dublin and then to Liverpool, England. Liverpool was a port of departure for thousands of emigrating Irish people. In 1850 alone, 159,840 Irish people departed from Liverpool for the United States. The Eagans boarded the *Caroline Nesbit*, and after weeks at sea, John and his mother landed in New York City on August 15, 1850.

New York City was crowded with emigrants from European countries. Irish immigrants comprised one quarter of the city's population of half a million people. John found work as a hack driver and drove the hack for eighteen months, until he had saved enough money to move out of New York City. John and his mother left for Michigan the next year. They traveled to Flint, in Genesee County. John found work in the newly established foundry of King and Forsyth, where he learned the trade of blacksmithing. He stayed with King and Forsyth for two years. Afterward, John went on the road as a journeyman blacksmith. There were hundreds of blacksmiths all over Michigan. They worked from dawn to dusk, six days of the week. Horseshoes were among the most important items they made, but they also produced household goods like pots, pans, door latches, nails, spikes, shovels and farm implements. John carried all of his tools with him.

Two years later, John Eagan opened his own blacksmith shop. The shop was located in Pine Run, a small village in Vienna Township. He kept the shop for three years. While living in Pine Run, John met and married Caroline Hinkley. They began a family but saw a number of their children die in infancy. In 1858, John decided to move his business to the town of Flushing. John operated this forge for nearly twenty years. He left blacksmithing only when ill health forced him to lay down his tools. Working in a forge had its dangers—flying pieces of metal could blind a person, the persistent noise from the hammering of the anvil could deafen, and working indoors in poorly ventilated rooms damaged lungs. John turned to manufacturing wagons and sleds. After this, he worked in the grocery business.

In 1882, John purchased 156 acres of land in Mount Morris Township, Genesee County. He brought nearly all of the land under cultivation, either in grain or orchard crops. He began to raise stock cattle. The family home included his wife and mother and three children. John Eagan lived to see the dawning of a new century, and a few years beyond, until 1912. The tools of his trade, the hammer and the anvil, helped him to forge a new life in America.

26

GLADWIN COUNTY

What's for Breakfast?

J ames Riley came to America from Ireland in 1850 at the age of twenty-two. His first ten years were spent working at various jobs that brought him eventually to Michigan in 1860. James traveled first to Saginaw, where the great lumbering boom was in full swing. Saginaw County was the hub for lumbering due to the many rivers flowing into Lake Huron. Thousands of logs were floated along the rivers to port towns, then loaded onto ships for export. From Saginaw, James continued on through dense forest covered in pine and oak trees.

In Midland County, James was hired as a cook for one of the camps owned by the L.B. Curtis Lumber Company. His day began at 4:00 a.m., when preparations for the lumbermen's breakfast began. At 6:00 a.m., the men streamed into the camp dining area. They were served bacon, eggs, fried potatoes, pancakes, fruit and toast. The men ate as much food as they could as quickly as they could. There was no talking allowed at breakfast time.

Once the lumbermen, or shanty boys as they were known, left for the woods, breakfast was cleared away. James immediately began preparing the men's next meal, to be served at 11:30 a.m. Usually, the men stayed out in the forest all day, so their second meal had to be carried out to them. James prepared and packed a lunch for each worker. The meal consisted of three meat sandwiches and a sweet cake or fruit. Once the lunches were on their way to the men, James began preparing the evening meal. This meal was also hearty, with roast beef or pork, vegetables and biscuits and plenty of hot tea and coffee. There was plenty of work in the kitchen all day long.

Lumber camp cook's shanty. *Michigan State University Archives and Historical Collections.*

The daily baking of bread, pies, cookies, cakes and doughnuts took hours. James was never off duty before 8:30 p.m. Keeping the lumbermen fed was a monumental task. But the compensation was worth it. As a cook, James was one of the highest paid workers in the camp, earning as much as three dollars per day.

A lumberman was only as good as the food that he had in him. The shanty boys worked ten to twelve hours each day in all kinds of weather. They did not work unless they were well fed. The living conditions in the camp were rough and basic. There was a bunkhouse, the cook's shanty, the blacksmith shop, the camp office and a camp store. The camp foreman had his own house where he and his family lived. There might be anywhere from sixty to one hundred men in a camp. The only aspect of camp life that the lumbermen had any say over was their food. A camp without a cook, or a camp with a poor cook, did not survive. Fortunately, James turned out to be a wonderful cook. The lumbermen were pleased with his efforts. James could not have carried out all of the cooking preparations and the serving of meals on his own. He had assistance in the kitchen from young women hired by the company and some of the men's wives. One of James's helpers was seventeen-year-old Ruby Eldridge. She and James decided to marry in 1876.

James Riley had saved the money he earned as the camp cook, and he used his savings to buy eighty acres of land north of the town of Gladwin, in Gladwin County, Michigan. The land had already been cleared of trees. Only scrub brush and stumps remained. James cleared the land and put in crops of wheat, oats and barley. He began raising his own stock. He built a house for Ruby and their six children. Eventually, a road was built that cut through the Riley farm. On a daily basis, people, goods and animals passed by. When the railroad came along, even more people, goods and animals took up residence.

James lived to be nearly one hundred years old. He was known as the last of the first residents of Gladwin County, a true pioneer and a very good cook.

27

GOGEBIC COUNTY

A Prospector's Perspective

Richard Langford was born in Ireland in 1826. He set out for America in 1847, when he was twenty-one years old. Five years later, Richard arrived in Ontonagon County, Michigan, where he took up trapping and hunting. The area around Ontonagon had been written about since the mid-1600s, when large deposits of copper were found along the Lake Superior shoreline. Surveyors and geologists, as well as prospectors, were drawn to the site. In 1840, Dr. Douglas Houghton, the state geologist, visited the region and prepared a report detailing the extent of copper resources and iron ore in the area. His report suggested there was iron ore underneath the Gogebic Ridge straddling the boundary between the state of Michigan and the Wisconsin Territory.

Whenever Richard was out, he remained alert to visible signs of ore. One day in 1868, Richard sunk a test pit into the ground. The pit was not deep enough to strike ore, but Richard felt sure that iron ore was there. He returned to the same location three years later. This time, Richard saw iron ore lying on the ground beneath a fallen tree. He was determined to show some ore samples to men who might invest in a mine at this spot. He was not able to interest anyone for a number of years. Finally, in 1880, Richard met a man named Nat Moore, an Irish immigrant mining captain. When Captain Moore saw Richard's samples, he said that the ore should be tested for purity. The ore tested at high quality. Captain Moore walked to a land office in Wausau, Wisconsin, where he obtained the mineral and property rights to the area where the ore had been found.

Richard Langford believed that he was entitled to a quarter share of the Colby Mine, which opened at the site in 1884. The ore had been discovered on Colby Hill. In the first year, 1,022 tons of iron ore were taken from the mine. The news spread quickly that there was work for miners. Daily trains brought in hundreds of people to the area. Richard found himself left out, as Captain Moore disputed Richard's claim that he had found the first ore samples. Richard set off once more, alone and none the richer. He later said, "While others were accumulating wealth, I spent my time and what money I could get hold of in prospecting the minerals of this locality. My labors have brought wealth to others and me to the poorhouse. I could have established my right to a one quarter interest in the Colby Mine but I did not care to take such a step."

In the next year, another seven iron mines opened on the Gogebic Range. Overnight, small collections of cabins and shanties became towns. Mine company owners posted bulletins in many European countries, advertising good paying jobs. The cost of the voyage across the ocean would be paid for by the mining companies in return for a fixed number of years' work. So

Norrie Iron Mine, Gogebic County. *Victor F. Lemmer Papers, Bentley Historical Library, University of Michigan.*

many immigrants arrived, land for a new county, Gogebic, was taken from Ontonagon County.

The life of the miners in these boomtowns was not for Richard. He remained on his own, wandering through the woods. He was dubbed the "Hermit of Gogebic County," but Richard kept himself out of trouble throughout his lifetime. He was proud of the fact that he was a law-abiding citizen. He once said, "I have never had a lawsuit, been arrested, served as a witness or juryman. In fact, I have never been put under oath."

The mining boom in Gogebic County lasted from 1884 until 1958. In those seventy-five years, 245 million tons of iron ore were shipped to steel mills around the United States. Richard passed his remaining years in the area until ill health overcame him. Without any funds, and eventually blind, Richard was moved to the Ontonagon Infirmary, where he died at eighty-three years of age in 1909. Near the spot where he first saw the iron ore that begat the mining boom, a memorial plaque marks this immigrant prospector's life: "1,000 feet south, iron ore was discovered on the Gogebic Iron Range by Richard Langford about 1880."

28

GRAND TRAVERSE COUNTY

What Farming Was All About

Timothy Egan was born around 1834 in the south of Ireland, and he barely survived the potato famine years. When he had enough money, he decided to immigrate to Canada. From Canada, Timothy made his way to Michigan. He married Bridget O'Connor, and the two made their home in Grant Township in Grand Traverse County. After they settled there, other members of the Egan family found their way to Grant Township as well. Thomas Egan arrived in 1863. Patrick Egan arrived in 1864. Ten years later, on the same day, all three Egan men each received 160 acres in land grants from the Traverse City, Michigan land office. The men had completed "Declarations of Intent" to become U.S. citizens. In Timothy's declaration, he wrote, "It is bona fide my intention to become a citizen of the United States and I renounce forever all allegiance and fidelity to each and every foreign prince, potentate and state of sovereignty whatsoever and particularly the Queen of Great Britain of whom I have been a subject."

The Egan families lived near one another. Their farms prospered, and their families grew to include children and grandchildren. In 1880, a State of Michigan Agricultural Census was taken along with the population census of that year. The agricultural census contained information about all of the farms in the state. The contents included the name of the owner, the number of acres and the cash value of the farm, the crops produced, as well as all other items produced, the number and value of all livestock and the value of any homemade items produced. Timothy Egan was listed as a farm owner in Grant Township with forty-five acres of tilled land (a definition which included fallow land as well as "grass in rotation, whether pasture or meadow"). During the 1879 growing season, Timothy had grown

1 acre of buckwheat which produced 20 bushels of crop, 3 acres of "Indian Corn" yielding 40 bushels, 12 acres of oats yielding 185 bushels, 12 acres of wheat yielding 45 bushels, and 2 acres of "Irish Potatoes" yielding 150 bushels.

He also had

5 acres of grassland mown, and 4 acres not mown. From these lands were harvested 7 tons of hay.

Also, there were 115 acres of "woodland and forest," and 1 acre described as unimproved land that was not growing wood. The value of the farm "including land, fences, and buildings" was $600. The value of farm implements and machinery was $80. Other information provided in the census included the following:

One "milch" cow and one other head of cattle."
No buying, selling, slaughtering of any cattle in 1879.
No cattle "died, strayed, been stolen and not recovered."
75 pounds of butter produced in 1879.
No milk from the cow sold or sent to "butter or cheese factories."
No cheese made on the farm itself
1 pig and 15 chickens (barnyard poultry) laid a total of 74 eggs in 1879.
No horses, asses, or mules owned to help with work.
Total value of livestock is $50.
Cost of "building and repairing" fences on the farm is $20.
No cost claimed for fertilizer or hired labor in 1879.
Value of all farm productions (sold, consumed, or on hand) for 1879 is $339.
50 cords of wood cut.
Total value of all forest products sold or consumed in 1879 is $45.

The amount of work required to keep Timothy's farm going was more than one man with a wife and six children could manage. There were not any hired farmhands. One ancient Irish tradition the Egans brought with them from Ireland, was the Meitheal (a Gaelic word pronounced meh-hel). In this tradition, relatives and groups of neighbors helped one another out when it came to the big farming jobs such as saving hay, harvesting crops and caring for animals. Machinery was shared within the group. No one received any pay, other than their food while working. With the Meitheal, poor immigrants could build their homes and farms and were able to make them stable, even prosperous. The Egan families and their neighbors worked together. They all knew what farming was all about.

GRATIOT COUNTY

Irishtown, The Town that Never Was

After Congress passed the Graduation Act in 1854, there was a surge in westward movement by newly arrived immigrants. The government needed the income from land sales and wanted unimproved land made more valuable by having it converted to agricultural use. In 1855, a group of Irish immigrants trekked across the state of Michigan and found their way to a territory that eventually became known as Gratiot County. The area was full of white pine, tamarack trees in swampy ground and hardwood timber. The men were eager to take advantage of the inexpensive land prices. Among the first to buy were Patrick Murray, Michael Murray, Fergus Connelly, John Manion and Timothy Battle. They arrived early in the year, followed soon after by Patrick Egan and Thomas McLaughlin. Each staked a claim for 160 acres and had to live on his property for eighteen months in order to receive the price of fifty cents per acre.

The men settled in the townships of Lincoln, Coe and Seville. After clearing some of the land, the men began sending for their families to join them. A community began to form. These founding families were devout Catholics even though there was not a Catholic church anywhere nearby. The nearest church with a priest was in the town of Ionia, fifty miles away. The faithful walked or rode horseback those fifty miles in order to attend Mass. When the first baby, Patrick Connelly, was born in the settlement, on Christmas Day 1855, his mother carried him forty miles in order to have him baptized in a church in Westphalia, Michigan.

St. Patrick's Church, Irishtown. *Dorothy Mallory Collection. Artist's rendering courtesy of Tricksy Wizard Comics.*

More Irish families arrived during the next ten years. The settlement came to be known as Irishtown. There was neither a post office nor any local government. The one thing the settlers wanted was their own church. In 1868, a committee was formed to discuss the idea of building a Catholic church in Irishtown. Patrick Egan, Edmond Duggan, Fergus Connelly, Michael Murray and John Manion all served on the building committee. Property was donated by Roger Battle for the new church, and on July 4, 1868, construction began. The parishioners organized a log hewing bee, and the framework for the church began to take shape. Construction was completed in 1870. The new church was named Saint Patrick's after the patron saint of Ireland. St. Patrick's was a mission church, under the auspices of the larger Saginaw Catholic Church. Father Richard Sweeney usually rode his horse each month to Irishtown to celebrate Masses and officiate at baptisms, marriages and other services.

The mission, at times, floundered. Without a resident pastor, regular church services became a problem. However, many more immigrants were making their way into the mid-Michigan area. Many of these people were also devout Catholics. The church in Irishtown was now too small to accommodate all of its parishioners. The original building committee convened again in 1897. It was time to build a larger church. The cornerstone was laid during the summer of 1898, and the new church was completed in 1900. The dedication for the new church was held on June 14, 1900.

St. Patrick's was the center of Irishtown. Two miles east of Irishtown was the community of Summerton, which had a post office, a general store, a blacksmith shop, a Patrons of Industry Hall and a lodging place for travelers. Both Summerton and Irishtown seemed poised to continue growing as the new century began. There were plans for a railroad station, which would bring more people and commerce to the area. Alas, the railroad was built two miles east of Summerton, leaving it and Irishtown isolated and out of the way. The church remained the hub of the community. Saint Patrick's holds the memories of Irishtown in the names of the founding members etched into stained glass, in the handiwork of the local people who built the church and in the cemetery that serves as the final resting place for those courageous immigrants who first found their way to Irishtown.

30

HILLSDALE COUNTY

Fleeing the Famine

The Great Hunger in Ireland was a culmination of years of potato crop failure. The people living in the west of Ireland suffered greatly, especially between 1845 and 1850. In County Clare, Thomas McDonough, from the parish of Killmacsherry, and Mary Dwyre, from the parish of Kilmanahine, married during this difficult time. Mary gave birth to their son, John, on February 24, 1848. Thomas and Mary had only just survived the previous year, known as the "plague year." They decided to immigrate to America rather than go into a workhouse. People crawled into workhouses with their last vestiges of strength. Most were not only starving but also suffering from diseases. Four miles from the McDonough house was the Ennistymon Workhouse. The structure was built to accommodate 870 residents. During the worst years of the famine, new residents numbered 600 per month.

Thomas, Mary and John traveled to Liverpool, England, where they planned to immigrate to the United States. Here they met with difficulty due to the Passenger Acts recently passed by the U.S. Congress. The Passenger Acts limited the number of immigrants arriving in New York City and Boston, as the cities were ill-equipped to deal with the number of people coming ashore. The price of passage to America was raised to seven English pounds, double what the fare had previously been. The McDonoughs decided to sail to Quebec because the fare was three pounds, ten shillings. The ship was overcrowded, and unsanitary conditions led to the spread of dysentery and typhus, from which many did not recover. Those who did

Irish immigrant sailing ship. *Artist's rendering courtesy of Tricksy Wizard Comics.*

not recover were slid from the ship into the ocean. The voyage lasted eight weeks. Finally, the ship docked at Grosse Ile, one of the islands in the Saint Lawrence Estuary. Grosse Ile served as a quarantine station for immigrants bound for Quebec.

In 1847, 441 ships from the British Isles docked at Grosse Ile. Some 5,000 passengers died during the crossings, and another 2,200 dead were taken from the ships upon arrival. Those who died within nineteen miles of Grosse Ile were allowed to be ferried to land rather than slid overboard. Doctor George M. Douglas was the chief medical officer on Grosse Ile. He and his team examined the newly arrived immigrants and placed them in quarantine. They examined over 90,000 immigrants during the year. Many people died while in quarantine. There was an epidemic of typhus that killed medical personnel as well as immigrants.

It was thirty miles from Grosse Ile to Quebec City. From Quebec, the family made their way across the border into New York, settling in Monroe County. Thomas took up farming and also worked as a stonemason. Stonemasonry paid well, so Thomas was able to save some money. In 1852, he sent for his father to come to New York. The McDonoughs remained in Monroe County for fifteen years.

In 1865, the family decided to move to Michigan. Good farming land was available at affordable prices, so the McDonoughs traveled to Jefferson Township in Hillsdale County. John stayed with his parents until he reached the age of twenty-two. By then, he had enough money to purchase land for his own farm. John and Jane Whalen, of Lenawee County, married in 1875. John owned more than one hundred acres, which he brought under cultivation. He built a house and barns for storage and cattle. Together, he and Jane raised seven children. John McDonough passed away on Christmas Day, 1914. He was sixty-six years old. His lifelong dedication to his family and farm ensured that his children never experienced hunger.

31

HOUGHTON COUNTY

A Life of Service

Alice Ryan was born on January 22, 1855, to John C. and Johanna O'Donnell Ryan. In 1844, her father and his two brothers had emigrated from Limerick Junction in County Tipperary, Ireland. They first settled in the lead mining district of Wiota, Wisconsin. Alice's father tried farming, but after a few years, he decided to move to Houghton County, Michigan, where copper mining was expanding. His brothers soon joined him. John and Johanna married in 1854 and settled in the town of Hancock. After Alice, four more children were born.

In 1855, there was no Catholic church in Hancock, so Alice was baptized by Bishop Frederic Baraga in nearby Houghton. When she was eleven years old, a group of Sisters of St. Joseph of Carondelet from St. Louis, Missouri, traveled to Hancock to open a school. As soon as St. Anne's opened its doors, Alice was enrolled. Her parents wanted their daughter educated by the sisters.

After her high school graduation, Alice felt called to join the sisters. In 1873, she entered the Troy, New York Province of the Sisters of St. Joseph. On March 19, 1876, Alice made her final profession, officially accepting her vocation as a sister. She relinquished her name and became Sister Agnes Gonzaga.

For the next eleven years, Sister Agnes taught in schools in Troy and Glen Falls, New York. In 1885, she became the mother superior of a convent in Glen Falls. That same year, Mother Agnes received word of her father's death. She was unable to travel back to Hancock and so sent a telegram that

Franklin Copper Mine tramway. *Authors' collections.*

read, "I cannot come. Goodbye, father. Thank-you. I'll meet you in heaven." Two years later, she was assigned to Albany, New York, and appointed superintendent of schools for the order.

In 1893, Sister Agnes moved to Denver, Colorado, where she was a school principal for three years. Her brother William and her sister Julia were already living there. Both were in ill health, hoping the change of place would cure them. Her brother John was also in Denver but moved to Montana. In 1896, Sister Agnes learned that she had been elected to the General Council of the Sisters of St. Joseph, located in St. Louis, Missouri. Nine years later, Sister Agnes was elected superior general of the entire U.S. congregation of sisters. She was now the administrator of five hundred hospitals, fifty women's colleges and more than six thousand Catholic schools serving nearly two million children. Additionally, she oversaw orphanages, private academies, homes for the elderly and homes for unmarried mothers.

In 1900, Sister Agnes realized that her sisters needed further education and training in improved methods of nursing and teaching and childcare. She raised the salaries that sisters earned so they could take advantage of educational opportunities. She resisted pressures to be subservient to priests and other clerics. She responded to a priest who wrote to her that the sisters in his parish refused to clean his house. "The Rule of the Order forbade Sisters to provide housekeeping to priests. Find your own housekeeper!" was her reply.

Sister Agnes Gonzaga Ryan. *Sisters of St. Joseph of Carondelet–St. Louis Province Collection.*

In January 1908, Sister Agnes traveled to Rome, where she was granted a private audience with Pope Pius X. Later in the month, she was present at the beatification of Joan of Arc. When she returned to the motherhouse, she made plans to have a college built nearby for young women. A charter for the college was approved on April 17, 1917. Shortly thereafter, Sister Agnes retired as superior general, citing ill health. Two months later, she passed away.

Sister Agnes's death and World War I put building plans on hold. After the war, however, ground was broken for the women's college. John Ryan contributed funds so that five buildings could be completed. The college, Fontbonne University, opened in 1925. People wanted the administration building named for John Ryan, and he and his sister Margaret attended the dedication ceremonies for Fontbonne University. John demurred at having any building named for him. Instead, he professed that he wanted a building named for his sister, who had lived her life in service to others.

32

HURON COUNTY

A Humanitarian First, A Politician Second

John Murphy, the son of Irish emigrants from County Mayo who had fled the famine, was born in Guelph, Ontario. He studied law at the University of Michigan, graduating in 1879. Looking for a town in which to set up his practice, John came to Sand Beach, in Huron County. In 1885, John married Mary Brennan. Mary, born in Whitehall, New York, in 1867, was the daughter of emigrants from County Kilkenny, Ireland. She was a devout Catholic and generous to all. John and Mary found a house in town with room for children and an office for John. When their three sons and one daughter were born, Mary raised them to be polite, civic-minded and service-oriented citizens.

William Francis "Frank" Murphy was born on April 13, 1890. The Murphy household was cheerful, with a focus on education and regular attendance at Sunday Mass. After graduating from high school, Frank enrolled in the University of Michigan, graduating in 1914 with a degree in law. During the summer, Frank worked in the Huron Flour Mills, where his pay went toward his tuition and gave him pocket money. Frank noticed, however, that his same pay was all that other men with families earned at the mill, forcing them and their families to lead impoverished lives.

Frank went to Detroit and worked as a trial lawyer for three years. At night, Frank taught school in an immigrant neighborhood. He came to understand what he called the "submerged majority," all those who were trying to forge new lives in America. When the United States declared war on Germany, Frank enlisted. He was sent to Reserved Officers Training

Mary Brennan Murphy and Frank Murphy. *Bentley Historical Library, University of Michigan.*

Camp and was commissioned as a first lieutenant. He was a member of the American Expeditionary Force sent to France. Frank arrived on the day the armistice was announced and served in postwar Germany before sailing home to Michigan in July 1919. He received a federal appointment, first assistant U.S. attorney for the Eastern District of Michigan. He won all of the cases he prosecuted but one. In 1922, Frank resigned in order to open a law practice with a partner.

One year later, Frank was elected a judge in Detroit Recorder's Court. He was progressive in his thinking and fair-minded. He became well known nationally when he presided over two murder trials that involved the African American community. Judge Murphy was unprejudiced toward the African American defendants, which made headline news and endeared Frank to the people of the city. He was elected mayor of Detroit in 1930 during the Great Depression when 100,000 Detroit workers were unemployed. Frank promised assistance, and he rallied the mayors of other cities to demand federal aid for people suffering and in dire need.

Frank Murphy supported Franklin D. Roosevelt, who was campaigning for the presidency. He gave speeches encouraging people to "get behind Roosevelt" and had aspirations to join Roosevelt's administration. When Roosevelt was elected in 1932, Frank was appointed governor general of the Philippines. He served in this capacity for three years.

Frank lived in the governor's mansion in Manilla. His sister was the official first lady since Frank was unmarried. She presided alongside Frank at state dinners and formal functions. Frank noticed the disparity between his lifestyle and that of most of the Philippine people. He championed women gaining the right to vote and advocated fair laws for everyone. He supported Philippine self-governance by negotiating a treaty naming the Philippines a commonwealth of the United States for ten years only. Frank then served as high commissioner of the Philippines.

President Roosevelt was reelected in 1936, and he supported Frank for governor of Michigan. Frank won the election. At the beginning of 1937, workers at the General Motors Company in Flint staged a sit-down strike for better working conditions. Violence erupted, and the company owners demanded the national guard brought in to remove the striking workers. Governor Murphy sent the national guard to Flint, not to remove the men, but to maintain peace and ensure the strikers' safety. Eventually, Governor Murphy successfully negotiated a deal between the workers and management.

In 1939, Frank was appointed attorney general of the United States. He served for one year and then was named a justice of the Supreme Court of the United States. Justice Murphy wrote a dissenting argument in the case *Karamatsu v. the United States*. The 1944 case arose from the removal of Japanese Americans in 1942 from their homes and interning them as enemies of the United States. Frank described the internment as "legalized racism." He defended conscientious objectors, Native Americans and religious dissidents. He wrote pamphlets in support of Jewish people interned by the Nazi government.

Supreme Court Justice Frank Murphy. *Frank Murphy Papers, Bentley Historical Library, University of Michigan.*

Frank served on the Supreme Court for nine years. Whenever he had an opportunity, he returned to Harbor Beach, formerly Sand Beach. He always stayed in the family home. His bedroom was kept for him just as he had left it years before. Frank Murphy passed away on July 19, 1949. Politics brought him prominence, but he was first and foremost a humanitarian.

33

INGHAM COUNTY

An Ohio Neighbor Finds Rest in Michigan

Patrick Shannon of County Donegal owned property in Ireland and was very wealthy. He left Ireland in the late 1700s, settling in the Kentucky territory. When the American War for Independence from England began in 1775, Patrick joined a regiment under the command of General George Washington. During the winter of 1777, Washington and his troops were encamped for six months at Valley Forge, Pennsylvania. There were twelve thousand men in the camp, and they were hungry, diseased and despairing. Patrick spent nearly all of his money on aid for the men. After the war, he had just enough money to secure passage back to Ireland for his wife and himself. He planned to sell his property and then return to America. While Patrick and his wife, Elizabeth, were in Ireland, their son Joseph was born.

The family returned to Kentucky. Joseph grew up and then moved to Fayette County, Ohio, where he served as an apprentice tanner for two years. He and Ruth Algire, a native of Fairfield County, Ohio, married. In 1826, Ruth gave birth to their son John. The family moved to Wyandot County, Ohio, where Joseph bought land and built a tannery. Two years later, Ruth died, leaving Joseph and John on their own. The indigenous Wyandot people lived near the Shannon home, and they welcomed Joseph and John into their village. John learned their customs and language. Eventually, the Wyandots conferred upon Joseph the title of chief.

John and his father moved to Fort Findlay in Hancock County, Ohio, in 1836. Joseph opened a supply store that served the small community. One day, Joseph and John were walking through the cemetery when Joseph dropped dead. The title of chief to the Wyandots passed to John, who was only ten years old. He was sent to live with an aunt in Delaware County, Ohio. He attended a log school for three months in the year. When he was sixteen, John passed the teacher's examination and began teaching. He enrolled in Granville College in nearby Licking County, using his teaching salary and working on the college farm to cover his tuition.

In 1850, John became a Methodist preacher. He left teaching in order to travel throughout northern Ohio. He rode on horseback, taking with him only what fit into his saddlebag. He conducted church services in schoolhouses and people's homes. Four years later, he married Lucy Bassett in Wood County, Ohio. Together, they raised four children.

When the Civil War began in 1861, John Shannon enlisted in the 100th Ohio Infantry, Company A, of the Northern army. He was made a captain. Two years later, he was promoted to the rank of major and received an honorable mention for bravery. In September 1863, John was commanded to build fortifications around the town of Knoxville, Tennessee. There were not enough troops available for the work, so John was ordered to employ local African Americans to build the fortifications. He was then ordered to organize a regiment of African Americans to handle heavy artillery. The men were the First United States Colored Heavy Artillery. John was concerned with the men's welfare and their families who joined them in camp. He wrote a letter two months later to officials "requesting information in regard in providing for the families of those men….Some fifty families are now here and no adequate provision has either been made or authorized for them." John rose in rank to lieutenant colonel and then colonel.

Shortly after the war ended, while on duty in May 1865, John's horse fell, rolling over him. The bones in his chest were crushed. He was forced to retire from the army. John returned home, and he was admitted to the bar in Columbus, Ohio. He practiced law before the Ohio Supreme Court. He was then elected prosecuting attorney for Wood County. His years of practicing law were cut short when illness struck him. No longer able to work, John went to live with one of his married daughters in Ingham County, Michigan. The remaining years of his life were spent there until his death on November 30, 1894. Though John Shannon was a true-blooded Ohioan, Ingham County was his final resting place.

34

IONIA COUNTY

Mother Knows Best

Catherine Dwyer was born in Ireland in 1824. She was known as "Kitty" to her family and friends. Catherine married Patrick Davern, born in 1830 in Ireland. During the potato famine years, Kitty gave birth to two children. She and Patrick realized that the only hope for their survival was to leave Ireland. The family, including Kitty's mother and two sisters, made their way to Liverpool. While waiting for the ship, Kitty's mother became ill and was unfit to make the voyage. Kitty and the two children accompanied her mother back home. Patrick and the sisters would still make the journey. Patrick planned to find employment as soon as he reached America. He would save all of the money he could and then send for his family to join him.

When Patrick arrived in New York, he was amazed with all that he saw. America was new and bright and full of people just like him, eager to start a new life. All of the excitement caused Patrick to be rather slow in sending for the family to join him. Back in Ireland, Kitty's mother passed away. Kitty decided to sail on her own to meet Patrick in New York. She left her children in the care of relatives and booked her passage.

Kitty, too, was taken with her new country. She and Patrick found work on the Detroit and Milwaukee Railroad. The railroad company was laying tracks west through to the state of Michigan. Kitty baked bread and sewed shirts for the work crews. She and Patrick eventually saved enough money to buy land in Michigan, in the town of Pewamo, located in Ionia County. Once they owned their own land, Kitty sent for the children, along with one of her nieces to shepherd them to Michigan.

Kitty could neither read nor write, but she could do sums quickly. She was a tall, strong woman who could heft a barrel as well as any man. She was fiercely determined that her children would have better lives in Michigan than they ever could in Ireland. She worked to acquire as much land as she could afford and became known as an astute businesswoman. When the U.S. Civil War broke out in 1861, Kitty paid to have a substitute serve in Patrick's place. She did not want Patrick away from the family farm. Kitty knew Patrick to be a warm-hearted man who sometimes enjoyed the company of friends too heartily.

In 1868, the Davern family included three sons and three daughters. They did not escape their share of tragedies. One daughter died at the age of fourteen. Twenty-year-old Mary died from tuberculosis. A son, William, traveled to Des Moines, Iowa, to join an uncle living there but did not like his new residence. He wrote to Kitty, "Here I am and here I've got to stay." Kitty responded by sending William the train fare to return home. For the remainder of Kitty's life, she helped to make the town of Pewamo prosper. When the railroad arrived, it brought new settlers. A bank was built, and Kitty put up the money for the first brick building. She financed other buildings as well. Kitty Davern lived to the age of seventy-three. Upon her death in 1897, the executor of her will, the town banker, directed her last wishes to be fulfilled:

> *Be It Remembered, That I, Catherine Davarn* [most descendants use Davern], *of Dallas Township, Clinton County, Michigan, being of sound mind and memory, but knowing the uncertainty of this life, do hereby make, execute and declare this to be My Last Will and Testament, that is to say:*
> *I give and bequeath to my beloved husband, Patrick Davarn, the income from one thousand dollars during his natural life.*
> *I desire that my Executor look after my husband during his lifetime and see to it that he is provided with a comfortable house and necessary clothing. But in no wise to furnish him money to be squandered for drink or dissipation.*

All of Kitty's other assets and belongings were distributed among her children. Even in death, mother knew best.

35

IOSCO COUNTY

Till the Ground

Thomas Glendon was born in Toronto, Canada, in 1841. His parents were emigrants from County Kilkenny, Ireland. They settled in Toronto on their landing and remained there for twelve years. In 1853, the growing family had saved enough money to buy land in Tecumseh, Ontario. They began to clear and farm their land. They did not mind the grueling, long hours because this was their own land. They had been tenant farmers back in Ireland; owning their own land was its own reward. After a few years, the family sold this property and moved to the settlement at Walpole, about twenty-five miles from Tecumseh. Here, they farmed for another ten years.

Michael Glendon, Thomas's older brother, and Thomas, shared a deep affinity for each other. In 1863, the two young men crossed over the border between Canada and Michigan. They made their way across the state to Berrien County, near Lake Michigan. They found work in a lumber camp for six months. Afterward, Michael wanted to move closer to Lake Huron. He traveled to the small settlement of Tawas, in Iosco County. Ten years earlier, a wealthy politician named Gideon O. Whittmore bought five thousand acres of white pine land. He saw the potential for harvesting the forests. He built a steam sawmill in the midst of the forested land, and this was followed by the building of a mill, a dock, a general store, a post office, and houses for lumbermen. By the time Michael arrived, there were about 160 people living in and around Tawas. Michael found the working conditions much better in Tawas, so he sent for Thomas to join him. He traveled back home to Canada the following year so that he could bring his parents to Tawas as well.

Michigan white pine tree. *John Penrod–Penrod/Hiawatha.*

Michael, Thomas and their parents each took up quarter sections of adjacent land in Baldwin Township. Each section was 160 acres. People began to refer to the Glendon land as Glendon Settlement. In order to clear the land, thousands of pine and hemlock trees were burned. At the time, sending the felled trees to the mill was too costly. Their property was located on a road that was accessible only by a team of oxen or horses in the wintertime. During that first winter, Thomas worked for George O. Whittmore in his lumber camp. When springtime came around, he joined a construction crew working on a sawmill dock for another lumber company.

It took seven years for Thomas to bring his land under tillage. To supplement his income, he worked as a tail sawyer in lumber mills in Tawas and East Tawas. His farm became known as one of the best in Baldwin Township. Thomas had big plans for starting an orchard. He cleared twenty acres and then planted one thousand apple trees. He hoped to become a commercial grower of apples. His goal was to sell one thousand bushels of apples annually. Due to unfavorable weather, Thomas did not realize a profit with his apple harvest. He did exhibit apples at the Iosco County Fair, which drew the attention of men interested in buying his orchard land, but Thomas was unwilling to sell.

In 1868, Thomas and Lucy Earl married. Together, they raised seven children. Thomas continued to improve his farm while the children were growing up. Twenty-seven years later, in 1895, Thomas finally agreed to sell his orchard. The buyer was a Dr. Gates, from East Tawas, a man who bred horses. Gates offered to exchange farmlands with Thomas plus pay him an additional $700 for the orchard. Thomas agreed to the deal. He, Lucy and the children now owned a farm of 240 acres. Thomas built a spacious home for his family that he called The Pines. There was plenty of grazing land for his cattle, horses and sheep. He kept his fields tilled and planted with the help of his son Richard. Thomas took on some civic duties within the township, serving as a school trustee and township supervisor. First and foremost, Thomas was a farmer. His heart was in the ground he tilled until the day he died in 1919.

36

IRON COUNTY

Three Men of Iron County

The town of Iron River had its share of memorable characters during the mid-1800s. Lewis Reimann, in his memoir recalling growing up in Iron County, *Between the Iron and Pine*, wrote about three men who made a great impression on him.

Paddy O'Toole came to Iron River from County Cork, Ireland. He lived in the town with his family. Paddy was the town marshal and the pound master. As pound master, he was "responsible for the feeding and care of all of the stray livestock, such as hogs, cattle, horses, sheep and geese." It was unlawful for cows and horses to be wandering loose on the village streets, so Paddy rounded up stray animals and put them into an impound yard in a vacant lot near his home. Owners paid Paddy a fine, determined by himself, in order to have their animals released. Many farmers drove their cattle through the town to a common pasture at the other end of the town in the morning and then retrieved them in the evening. On many occasions, Paddy locked up these animals in transit. Annoyed farmers argued with Paddy, but it did them no good. Instead, the farmers waited until Paddy left to round up more strays. Then they opened the enclosure, allowing the animals out again. Paddy's brother, Mike, who sided with the farmers, helped.

Paddy was appointed the property tax collector when the town officials decided to begin collecting those taxes. Many local merchants were opposed to property taxes and refused to pay. Paddy drove his horse and dray along Main Street, stopped in front of a shop, climbed down and went inside to collect the tax money. If the owner would not pay, Paddy began removing items from the store shelves and piling them into his dray. "Just pay your taxes! Pay your taxes and say nawthin!" Paddy was heard to shout.

Pat Kelly's general store was located on the main business corner of the town. Looking into the front store windows, one could see piles of goods. There were "horse collars, mackinaws, straw hats, a barrel churn and variety of work clothing." Inside, one side of the store displayed piles of underwear, shirts, hats, jackets and tools such as a man would need. The other side showcased the groceries along a counter. Customers could purchase "salt meat, tobacco, pipes, cheeses, candy and gum." There was a big red coffee grinder at one end of the counter. In front of the counter "were tin bins holding rice, oatmeal, cornmeal, sugar, and other foods scooped out and measured on a scale." Calendars from years past decorated the back wall, along with harnesses, pails and lanterns and other tools. In the middle of the store was the pot-bellied stove, the focal point of the whole place.

Vociferous political debates took place in the store. Pat maintained neutrality but allowed everyone to have his say. In the wintertime, the older men met daily around the stove. In the summertime, a long plank ledge alongside the front of the store served as a cool spot for their meetings. Upcoming elections and candidates were discussed late into the night.

Jim Murphy, born in Canada to Irish parents in 1868, came to Iron River in 1886. He was a well-respected and skilled timber estimator. He was in high demand among the big lumber companies and would set off into the woods "with a compass, a small cruiser's ax, a blanket, a rifle, a small sack of flour, a tin of tea and a slab of bacon." He might be away for weeks at a time. Jim could walk through a stand of pine trees, calculating mentally how many thousand feet of logs forty acres would produce. His word led the owners of lumber companies to buy huge tracts of timberland. When Jim first arrived in Iron County, the land was covered in pine trees. By the time he retired, the land was bereft of trees and under cultivation for farming. "Those were great days. We had rough men and rough times, but I wouldn't trade them for the free and easy life people live now," Jim said as he neared the end of his days.

37

ISABELLA COUNTY

Choosing Your Words Wisely

M ichael and Bridget Flynn Bennett sailed to America in 1827. They were from the "County of Kings," County Offaly in Ireland. Michael and Bridget settled in Pennsylvania, where Michael took up farming. They remained in Pennsylvania for four years. In 1831, Michael sold their property in order to claim a homestead in the Michigan Territory. Michael's claim of eighty acres was located in Northfield Township, in Washtenaw County. As one of the early landowners, Michael helped to build the first church.

Michael sold the farm in Northfield in 1837. He moved his family to Deerfield Township in Livingston County, where he bought a half section in the township. Two years later, a son Cornelius was born. When Cornelius was old enough, he worked on the farm and attended school. At age seventeen, Cornelius took up studies in Ann Arbor. After eighteen months, he was qualified for teaching. Cornelius spent the next winter teaching but then had a yen for adventure.

In the spring of 1858, Cornelius signed on with a construction convoy heading to the western outpost of Leavenworth, Kansas. The crew would build forts in the Sonora Territory where soldiers were stationed. When the convoy was approaching Salt Lake City, Utah, they received word from the Mormon congregation forbidding them passage through the city. To prevent the convoy's progress, the grazing fields leading to Salt Lake had been destroyed. Without an adequate supply of food for the oxen, they could not continue. The convoy turned around and headed back to Leavenworth.

Back in Leavenworth, Cornelius joined a supply train. He was given charge of the first wagon train heading to Denver, Colorado. There were twenty-eight wagons loaded with army supplies and mining supplies. It took Cornelius two months to convey the wagon train to Denver. During the journey, the most serious obstacles arose from the jealous temperaments of some of the men. With a careful choice of words, Cornelius diffused difficult situations.

Denver was in the midst of gold fever, leading Cornelius to form a partnership with a miner. They worked in three different mines. Once, Cornelius and his partner were asked to resolve a dispute between two miners. They sat down with one of the men to discuss the situation, and the man pulled out his pistol. Cornelius grabbed his arm before the gun could be fired. The two disputing miners then moved off by themselves to settle their argument. When they were out of sight, a shot was fired. All rushed to see what had happened. One miner was seriously wounded, and the other had fled. The miners were riled up. A shooter must hang. Since the shooter was gone, a substitute must be found, and it was Cornelius. Cornelius did not show any fear. Speaking slowly and calmly, he diffused the miners' tempers and saved his own life.

After this incident, Cornelius returned to Michigan. He studied at a seminary in the town of Howell for two years and worked as a clerk in the law office of S.F. Hubbell. He also enrolled in the University of Michigan to study law. On March 25, 1865, Cornelius graduated with his law degree. Two months later, he moved to the town of Mount Pleasant, in Isabella County, where he began his law practice. In 1869, a vacancy arose in the dual offices of county clerk and register of deeds for Isabella County. Cornelius was appointed to fill the vacancy. The next year, he was officially elected to the position, which he held for three more years. He also served as a justice of the peace and a probate judge.

Cornelius and three other men established a banking house known as Hicks, Bennett & Co. Cornelius then merged his law practice with the management of real estate. During this time, he also platted forty acres of land in the town of Mount Pleasant. Cornelius had married in 1865, but his wife, Mary Mosher, died at the age of twenty-nine. She left Cornelius with a young son. Cornelius married a second time in 1875 to Anna Palmer. They had two daughters, but only one survived childhood.

A yearning for learning carried Cornelius Bennett through life. Long before Cornelius was formally trained in the legal profession, he had learned that choosing his words wisely served himself and others best.

38

JACKSON COUNTY

Trained to Be an Engineer

On June 28, 1832, the Detroit and St. Joseph Railroad Company received a charter to commence building a railroad in the Michigan Territory. The Detroit and St. Joseph Railroad later became known as the Michigan Central Railroad. Construction and laying of tracks began in Detroit in 1836 with the initial line reaching the town of Ypsilanti by February 1838. The connection to Ann Arbor was completed in 1839. The line from Ann Arbor to Jackson, Michigan, was then completed on December 29, 1841. The Michigan Central and all of the other rail companies receiving charters had an immediate need for engineers and track layers.

Frank McDevitt was born in the town of Brighton, in Livingston County, Michigan, on September 7, 1855. His parents, Francis and Sarah Thompson McDevitt, were natives of County Derry in Ireland. Francis, born in 1810, was a blacksmith like his father, Daniel McDevitt. Daniel carried on the blacksmith trade throughout his entire adult life in Ireland. Francis served a five-year apprenticeship in Derry before immigrating to the United States in 1840. Upon his arrival in America, Francis came into New York City but did not settle there. Instead, he made his way to Hamburg Township in Livingston County. Francis easily found employment with his blacksmithing skills. In 1845, he married Sarah, his brother's widow. Francis was able to save enough money to purchase forty acres of land near the town of Hamburg, so the family moved there in order to take up farming.

As one of the younger children, Frank was able to receive a basic education. He attended school until the age of fifteen. Frank left Livingston County and began walking toward Chicago to seek his fortune. Frank arrived in Chicago in 1872. After trying his hand at various jobs, he decided that the big city was not the place for him. He traveled to Jackson, Michigan, where he found employment in the H.A. Hayden & Co. Aetna Flour Mills. Frank worked as a fireman in the engine room of the mill, and after two years, was promoted to the position of engineer. He worked at the mill for another four years. In 1877, Frank married Emma Cox. They had two children, a daughter, Edith, and a son, Frank.

After leaving the Aetna Mills, in 1878, Frank was hired by the Michigan Central Railroad. Initially, he worked as a fireman but then became an engineer for one of the company's trains. Frank continued working as an engineer until his retirement. His daily run took him from the town of Jackson to Michigan City, Indiana, and back. He was a reliable and safe operator. Fortunately for Frank, organized labor unions, such as the Brotherhood of Locomotive Engineers, established in 1863 by a group of Michigan Central engineers, campaigned vigorously for workers' rights regarding rail safety. In the earliest days of running trains, locomotive

Michigan Central Engine #86. *Bentley Historical Library, University of Michigan.*

engineers often found themselves working in difficult conditions, including twenty-four-hours shifts. When Frank joined the Michigan Central, he also joined the Brotherhood of Locomotive Engineers. The group was the first transportation organization formed in the United States. Frank also joined the Ancient Order of United Workmen, founded in 1868. This fraternal order was the first to offer life insurance to its members in the form of a death benefit paid to beneficiaries.

Beginning in the 1830s to 1910, over nine thousand steam railroad miles of track were in use in Michigan. In 1909, there were 81,695 people working on the steam railroads in Michigan. Frank McDevitt was one of those people trained to be an engineer.

39

KALAMAZOO COUNTY

An Adventurer Finds His Way Home

Edward Denniston was born at Coburg Lodge, in Roscommon County, Ireland, on March 2, 1821, to John and Alice Dowling Denniston. John Denniston's father was an Episcopal minister, and John intended to follow in his father's footsteps. Instead, when his father died, John was sent to live with his uncle, who directed him to take up farming. John bought his own farm when he and Alice married in 1820. When Edward was fifteen, the family decided to immigrate to the United States. Upon their arrival, they traveled to Northampton, Massachusetts, because John's brother Dr. D.D. Denniston was living there. John looked around for a suitable place to take up farming. He eventually chose Genesee County, New York.

Edward made his own plans once the family reached America. He chose to remain in Northampton with his uncle. He stayed for one year and, while there, attended the local secondary school. The following year, Edward accepted a position with another uncle, James Denniston, in New York City. James owned a dry goods jobbing house. Edward became a shipping clerk. Jobbers dealt in the wholesale selling of textiles, shoes, boots and all kinds of other goods. Edward worked for his uncle for two years. After that, he decided to strike out on his own.

Edward did not have much money so he walked to Buffalo, New York. He carried all of his clothes in a small bundle. When he reached Buffalo, he sold his one extra suit of clothes. He used the money to buy passage on a boat going to Detroit, Michigan. During the trip, Edward met a man who was heading for Schoolcraft, Michigan, and decided to travel with him.

When the two arrived in Schoolcraft, they parted ways. Edward walked to the village of Kalamazoo in Kalamazoo County. Kalamazoo was only a small clearing within vast acres of wilderness.

Edward was hired by a farmer who put him to work on the Indian Field. The pay was nine dollars per month. After twenty months, Edward bought eighty acres of land. He continued to hire himself out by the month for the next seven years. In 1847, Edward bought another eighty acres of land. This time, he improved the property and then sold it in order to move to Terre Haute, Indiana. Edward took a job there as a clerk and weigh master in a meatpacking firm. His contract in Terre Haute lasted for nearly two years.

In 1849, Edward caught gold fever. He traveled to California, arriving in June. There were thousands of determined men searching for gold, but Edward did not find any gold. Instead, he invested in a company that planned to divert the North Fork of the American River to expose the riverbed for mining. This enterprise was going along quite well until the spring floods came, overtaking the river's fork and washing away all traces of the mining works and the precious metal too. Edward lost all that he had invested.

Undaunted, Edward traveled to Sacramento, California. He borrowed money to purchase four yoke of oxen and a wagon. He started hauling miners and their supplies to their claims. Edward became a wealthy man. He decided to invest in $7,000 worth of cattle, which he stationed on a ranch at the head of the Sacramento River. Six months later, there was an ambush and the cattle were driven off. The financial loss was great, but Edward was able to buy more cattle and begin again. One month later, another ambush occurred. With only a few cattle, one horse and $1,000 remaining, Edward was finished with California.

Edward arrived in Kalamazoo in 1851 but did not remain. He bought land in Wisconsin, which he improved and then sold. In 1853, Edward came back to Kalamazoo, where he and Margaret Hawkins married on March 17. Margaret gave birth to four sons, and Edward bought farmland in Pavilion Township. He built a large frame house and several barns. Margaret passed away in 1871. He married again in 1873, this time to Lydia Beckwith. The remainder of Edward's life was lived on his farm in Kalamazoo County. The adventurer had found his way home.

40

KALKASKA COUNTY

Home on the Grange

Charles Murray was born in Waukesha County, Wisconsin, in 1847. When he was two years old, he and his parents moved across Lake Michigan into Montcalm County, Michigan. Elon and Ruth Murray had immigrated to the United States from Ireland. Elon Murray was in the mercantile business. After a few years, the family moved once again, this time to Ionia County. Charles was able to attend school and received what was considered a solid, basic education.

The lumber boom was on when Charles reached young adulthood, and he found employment in various sawmills. Eventually, he became head sawyer in a camp in Ionia County. At the age of twenty-one, he married Mary Raby of Washtenaw County, Michigan. They had one daughter. He continued as head sawyer until deciding to join his parents, who had moved north to Kalkaska County in 1883. His father was still in the mercantile business, a venture Charles decided to take on for himself.

Charles and Mary bought sixty acres of farmland in South Boardman Township, and they planted all of the crops that grew well in the area. The farm prospered. Both he and Mary became members of the Valentine Grange, Patrons of Husbandry. The Patrons of Husbandry was the official name given to an organization whose purpose was to assist rural farmers in all ways that they might need help. Another name for the organization was the National Grange. Oliver Kelley, a Department of Agriculture employee, along with six other founding members, created the organization on December 4, 1867, in Washington, D.C. This was soon followed by

An 1800s Michigan farm. *Authors' collections.*

states setting up chapters, then local communities organizing a chapter in their particular rural community. The State of Michigan Grange organized on April 15, 1873, in the village of Kalamazoo. Members of the grange "provide service to agriculture and rural areas on a variety of issues, including economic development, education, family endeavors and legislation designed to assure a strong and viable Rural America," according to its founders.

Members of a local Grange sometimes bought communal equipment, which they then shared through planting and harvesting time. When railroad companies began to charge high prices for storing grain before it was sent by rail to cities, Grange members began building their own grain elevators. Members were also vocal in calling for the government to step in to regulate the freight charges that railroad companies imposed.

One of the most unusual features of the National Grange and the state and county branches was that from the start, women were allowed to join as equal members among the men. The Grange also supported women's suffrage. Children were encouraged to become active in the Grange as well. Eventually, the children's branch became known as the Future Farmers of America.

The Grange was not just about the working needs of farmers. A Grange Hall was often the place where country dances, quilting bees and other social activities took place. The members supported one another. The communal fellowship and activities helped to relieve some of the tedium of rural life, with its continual daily routine of hard work, and the isolation that many living on farms, far from their neighbors, felt keenly.

Charles Murray served as treasurer of Boardman Township. He also served as the township clerk and supervisor. The remainder of his days were spent in his home, and on his farm, made possible by the Grange.

41

KENT COUNTY

Pulling Stumps, Planting Grain

Thomas Boylan was born in County Louth, Ireland, on April 15, 1827. His parents, Cornelius and Mary McCabe Boylan, were tenant farmers who married in 1823. The county of Louth was mostly agricultural land. In the 1830s, more than half of the Irish living there worked as farm laborers for landlords, many of whom owned vast estates. By 1834, there were four children in the Boylan family. Providing for them was a daily struggle. So, Cornelius and Mary decided to immigrate to America. Thomas Boylan was seven years old.

The family survived the ocean crossing to the port of New York City. From there, they traveled north to Seneca Falls, a town on the Seneca River, surrounded by forests. Men were needed for lumbering and for clearing deforested land of stumps and debris so the land could be sold for farming. Cornelius hired himself out as a laborer. The family stayed in Seneca Falls for ten years. Cornelius earned enough to keep his family fed, and he was able to save some money, too. In 1844, the Boylan family moved to Green Oak Township in Livingston County, Michigan. Michigan was covered in forests just as upper New York State had been. Cornelius once again hired himself out to clear land. His son Thomas, now seventeen years old, worked alongside him. The family stayed in Green Oak for eight years.

The Boylans then moved to Vergennes Township in Kent County. Thomas Boylan bought his own 160 acres in nearby Ada Township in 1861. Here, too, there were only stumps on the property. Thomas first dug around the stumps and then had to burn whatever his yoke of oxen could not pull free from the ground. Even with the stumps removed, sometimes several oxen were required to pull the plow through the ground. Thomas gained a good reputation among the other farmers in the county who admired his hard work and efficiency. His services were sought by other farmers to assist in clearing their own land.

In 1860, Thomas and Susan Murray married. Susan was the daughter of John and Mary Brady Murray. She had been teaching in a school in Ionia County for two years when she married Thomas. Thomas and Susan had eleven children, but two died while infants. Diphtheria took the lives of four more of their children, all within six weeks. The "contagion in the air" was second only to consumption, or tuberculosis, in lives claimed. Children under the age of ten were particularly susceptible. Often, the victims suffered from a painful, hoarse cough. Other organs, such as the heart, were sometimes affected. Many young children's last hours were spent in terrible agony before they suffocated and succumbed to the disease.

The Boylan land bordered the Grand River. Eventually, the Boylan farm became known as one of the best farms in the Grand River Valley. Thomas continued to hire himself out to his neighbors as their lands needed clearing and plowing. He also hired himself out for threshing days during harvest time. Thomas was the first in the county to introduce steam power for threshing grain. Before the steam-powered thresher, farmers threw the harvested grain crop into a hand-fed cylinder, which contained the grain, straw and chaff. Everything came out in a heap from the other end of the cylinder. The farmers would then use a pitchfork to pull away the straw. The grain and remaining chaff then went into a handheld winnowing machine pulled by a horse or the men. Thomas brought in a thresher powered by a portable engine. The power-driven thresher automatically separated the grain from the straw and chaff.

Thomas took pride in his farm and community. He helped build the first roads, schools and churches in the locality and served as a justice of the peace. Cornelius and Thomas pulled stumps and planted grain, ensuring the continuation of their farms into a new century.

42

KEWEENAW COUNTY

A Miner's Son

Patrick Henry O'Brien was born "near the Phoenix Mine, under the bluff, at the west vein" according to a Houghton County biographical article written about him when he was thirty-five years old. He was born on July 15, 1868, in Keweenaw County, Michigan. He was the son of Patrick J. O'Brien, an Irish immigrant from Glengariff, County Cork. Patrick arrived in Boston in 1856. In 1863, when Patrick was twenty-six years old, he heard about the mineral deposits being discovered in Michigan. Patrick traveled to Michigan and then headed north, to the shores of Portage Lake, which flowed into Keweenaw Bay and Lake Superior. Patrick was hired to work in the Cliff Mine. The Cliff Mining Company was established in 1845. It was the first copper company in the region. With the Civil War ongoing, the demand for copper was high due to its use in weapons manufacturing.

During this time, Patrick met and married Mary Harrington. Five children eventually completed their family. Patrick Henry was the second-born son. He did not become a miner like his father or older brother, Timothy. Instead, Patrick Henry went to school. He first attended school in Allouez, near the town of Phoenix. Then, he attended school in Osceola. He graduated with honors from Calumet High School in 1887. He then took a teaching position in the nearby town of Copper Harbor and also in Copper Falls. After two years of teaching, Patrick Henry enrolled in the Northern Indiana College at Valparaiso, Indiana. He planned to study law.

The following year, Patrick's father was killed in a mining accident at the Calumet and Hecla Mine where he had been working for three years.

Cliff Mine, oldest mine on Lake Superior. *Michigan Technological University Archives and Copper Country Historical Collections.*

The C&H Company was the leading producer of copper in Michigan and known for taking care of its workers. Patrick's family was financially stable because the C&H Company maintained an accident fund for its employees. Workers paid fifty cents every week into the fund, which the owners matched. The company also built a hospital for its employees. The C&H owners believed that contented workers were less likely to strike, so they provided their employees many benefits. The company provided worker housing in company towns and built schools and churches, an opera house, movie houses and a library. The library contained books in twenty different languages due to the diversity of the immigrant workforce.

With his mother and the rest of the family at home taken care of, Patrick Henry continued his studies. One year later, he was admitted to the bar on April 1, 1891. He began practicing law in West Superior, Wisconsin. His diligence and hard work paid off, making his practice profitable. Patrick Henry remained in West Superior for eight years. He and Elizabeth Kelly, known as Bessie, a native of Ottawa, Canada, married in 1897. Their first son was born two years later. Patrick Henry decided to return to his native place.

The O'Brien family moved to Laurium, Michigan, another C&H Company town, located in Houghton County. Patrick Henry served as

Above: Calumet &
Hecla Copper Mine
loading rocks. *Michigan
Technological University
Archives and Copper Country
Historical Collections.*

Left: Patrick O'Brien.
*Michigan Technological
University Archives and Copper
Country Historical Collections.*

the village attorney from 1901 until 1906. He continued his law practice as well. Three more children were born into the family. In 1912, Patrick Henry began officiating as a judge in the Twelfth Circuit Court. He was sympathetic to the grievances that copper miners had due to the paternalistic practices of the mining company owners. During the copper strike of 1913, Patrick Henry mediated between the miners and the company owners. He remained a judge for the next ten years. During his last term, Bessie passed away on January 14, 1921.

Patrick Henry married again in 1926. His second wife was Florence Elza Haas. Florence had two sons from her first marriage. The family moved to Detroit, where Patrick Henry often ran for public office. He was a candidate for the state senate, the U.S. House of Representatives, Supreme Court justice and governor of Michigan. He was not successful, but he did serve one term as the attorney general of Michigan from 1933 to 1934. He also became a probate judge for Wayne County in 1939. This miner's son practiced civic responsibility until his death at the age of eighty-eight in 1956.

43

LAKE COUNTY

The Mail Must Come Through

The time was ripe for rebellion in Ireland in 1798. The Irish Catholic population and other dissenters from the official Church of England were living under the Penal Laws. The United Irishmen planned large-scale uprisings in the provinces of Ulster and Leinster. Smaller factions of the brotherhood planned to confront the British soldiers in small towns and villages. One of the towns was Carlow, in County Carlow. Unbeknownst to the rebels, informants had alerted the British forces in Carlow about the uprising. British yeomen hid themselves inside homes in the town. When the rebels walked into the town center, they were ambushed. Greatly outnumbered, the rebels took refuge in other houses in the town. The soldiers set fire to these houses, trapping the people inside. Those who fled from the burning houses were shot. When there were only smoldering ruins remaining, there were more than five hundred dead. The rebellion was crushed.

John Doyle was born eight years after the rebellion, in 1806. He grew up in Borris, a village eighteen miles from Carlow. He heard the story of the massacre. When John reached adulthood, he bought passage on a ship sailing to Quebec, Canada, thankfully surviving the voyage. Upon reaching Quebec, he made his way to the small village of Hastings, in Northumberland County, Ontario.

In 1835, the village of Hastings had but one house. When a lock, as well as a dam and slides, was built at nearby Crooks Rapids, many men found employment. The village of Hastings grew to accommodate the influx of workers. During this time, John met and married Mary Theresa Leigh, another Irish immigrant. Together, John and Mary had six children. The children grew up in Hastings, where John and Mary ran a hotel.

One son, Dominick, born in 1846, remained in Hastings until he reached the age of nineteen. After the Civil War ended in 1865, Dominick crossed the border from Canada into Michigan, seeking employment in a lumber camp. He made his way to Oceana County, which was densely forested in white pine trees. Dominick found work in a small lumbering settlement known as Carr Settlement.

In addition to lumbering in the wintertime, Dominick volunteered to deliver mail from the post office in Pentwater, Michigan, twenty-eight miles away, to the settlers at Carr Settlement. Dominick became quite well known as he made this trek. He was a welcome sight for settlers who had no close neighbors. Dominick's journey began early in the morning. He walked to Pentwater, arriving at the post office in the afternoon. After collecting the mail and a short rest, Dominick began the walk back to Carr Settlement. He walked by moonlight along a forest trail. Dominick arrived back in Carr Settlement at daylight.

In 1872, Dominick married Louise (Lois) Brown. Their first son, John, was born the next year. Eight more children joined the family. The family home was in Lake County. Dominick continued working in a lumber mill where he was employed as a sawyer by J.S. Stearns, who had established a lumber mill on the Flint & Pere Marquette Railway a few miles east of the town of Ludington in Mason County. The Stearns Company supplied timber for the rebuilding of 17,500 homes that had been destroyed in the Great Chicago Fire in 1871. The company also supplied hardwood to build the Chicago Exposition. Dominick gained a reputation among the other lumbermen; few men wanted to work with him due to his strength and endurance. Stories circulated that he could run from tree to tree, applying the saw, without rest.

Eventually, all of the trees were felled. Employees of the Stearns Company were offered the option of buying the treeless land. After clearing the stumps, the land could be used for farming, so Dominick became a farmer. By 1900, he and his family occupied a farm in the village of Branch, Mason County, Michigan. Lois named their home "the little garden of Eden." Dominic set his mailbag down in order to pick up his plow. He remained a farmer until his life's end in 1914.

44

LAPEER COUNTY

A Bugler's Call

William Russell was born in County Sligo, Ireland, on February 26, 1842, to John and Mary Kane Russell. William was nine years old when his family immigrated to the United States. Mary Russell died soon after their arrival, and John married a second time. His second wife was Mary Taylor. She and John added four more children to the family.

In 1853, the family bought a farm of eighty acres in the town of Almont, in Lapeer County, Michigan. William, at age eleven, had already been employed for two years by a mechanic. His next job was assistant engineer to a man named Michael Kane who worked on a tugboat, the *R.R. Elliott*. William kept this position for another two years. After this, he spent five years working in a carriage factory.

In 1861, when the Civil War began, William volunteered with the First Michigan Cavalry, Company 1, as a bugler. Buglers were required to be eighteen years of age and played an essential role in the war. They sounded the time for daily duties in the camp, and bugle calls were used as a form of communication among troops during battles. Initially, drummers pounded out the directions the troops needed to follow. The beat of the drum, however, could not be heard over cannon fire.

William found himself in the thick of many battles. He and the other buglers served as messengers, surgical assistants and even on ambulance crews. Most buglers carried a rifle and fought with their companies. William found himself in charge of ninety-three men, fighting from Harper's Ferry to Winchester. He was captured during this battle and taken prisoner.

Michigan Infantry winter camp. *Michigan State University Archives and Historical Collections.*

Prisoners were often confined in extremely crowded conditions with few provisions or medical care. William spent time in Virginia prison camps in Lynchburg, Pemberton, Libby and Danville. The Lynchburg prison camp was on the site of the fairgrounds. The Danville prison camp was located in six tobacco warehouses; 4,500 Union soldiers were contained there. The warehouses had been stripped of all furnishings. There was a single pot-bellied stove for heat on each floor of the warehouse. Colonel A.S. Cunningham, Confederate States of America, upon inspection of the Danville camp, noted:

> *The prisoners at this post are in very bad condition, dirty, filled with vermin, little or no ventilation and there is an insufficiency of fireplaces.... It is a matter of surprise that the prisoners can exist in the close and crowded rooms, the gas from the coal rendering the air fetid and impure. The prisoners have almost no clothing, no blankets, and a very small supply of fuel....The mortality rate...about five per day, is caused, no doubt, by the insufficiency of food...and for the reasons stated above....This state of things is truly horrible.*

After the war, William returned home, one of the few from his regiment who survived. He decided to study medicine. William began his studies with a physician named Dr. McTaggart, who lived in Grand Rapids. In 1868, five veterans founded a college they named the Detroit Medical College. William began attending lectures there. Dr. Theodore McGraw and the other founders had experienced firsthand the horrors of war. Dr. McGraw focused on both teaching and involving his students in practical diagnosis. Under Dr. McGraw's tutelage, William qualified as a doctor.

Although he was quite busy with his medical studies, William and Agnes McKay married in 1868. Their son, Leland, was born one year later. Agnes was born in Kilmarnock, Scotland. She had come to the United States with her parents at a young age. Her father, William, owned a farm near William's father's farm in Almont Township.

After receiving his medical license, William returned to Lapeer County to set up his medical practice. Dr. William Russell was respected by his patients as well as his medical colleagues. He was elected president of the Saginaw Valley Medical Association and also became the U.S. examining surgeon in the region. He continued to practice medicine until his death in 1910. A bugler sounded the final notes at William's funeral.

45

LEELANAU COUNTY

A Cooper's Life Rolls Along

John and Alice Dorsey of County Kilkenny, Ireland, along with their infant son, John, immigrated to Canada in 1826. Three years later, John Dorsey died. Eventually, Alice married again. Alice, her husband and young John relocated to Michigan City, Indiana.

John's stepfather was a skilled cooper who taught John how to craft barrels. The family moved to Kenosha, Wisconsin. John attended the local school and then entered Notre Dame College planning to study for the priesthood. While he was there, John's mother died. He left Notre Dame and returned to Michigan City. He found work on sailing ships traveling back and forth between Michigan City and Chicago, Illinois.

In 1850, John was on a ship heading north on Lake Michigan. The boat came within sight of the four-hundred-foot sand cliff known as the Sleeping Bear as it entered the Manitou Passage. The boat came into a natural harbor at South Manitou Island. Local residents came to meet the boat, and John stepped ashore. There he met a man named John LaRue who lived on the island. John Dorsey mentioned that he was a cooper. LaRue was looking for a cooper to construct the barrels he needed for the fish and pelts he planned to ship to the Chicago markets. The two men agreed to work together. John returned to Michigan City to collect his tools and gear, arriving back on South Manitou Island in 1851.

John built a rough shack to live in and store his tools. He began gathering wood for constructing watertight barrels. John wanted the wood from oak trees because it was flexible. He first cut the wood for staves, which would form the body of a barrel. He inserted the staves into a bottom circular piece of wood, drawing them tightly together with a wooden hoop. He inserted the top end of the staves into the head of the barrel, again tightening them together with a hoop. When liquid was poured into the barrel, the staves expanded, making the barrel airtight.

Indigenous people caught the fish that John prepared for the Chicago market. Using salt and spices, the fish were preserved and then sealed into the barrels. The filled barrels were taken to the island dock and then loaded onto a boat. Eventually, John built his own cooper shop. He and LaRue also built a trading post and a general store near the harbor. John got along well with the local people. He was trustworthy and learned their indigenous language.

In 1855, a group of fourteen people arrived in Sleeping Bear Bay. They had sailed on board the SS *Saginaw*, the first steamer ship to land passengers in the settlement that became known as Glen Arbor. One of the passengers was fifteen-year-old Elizabeth Coggshall. John stepped forth to meet Elizabeth and to let her know that he intended to ask her to be his wife. When Elizabeth was sixteen, she and John married. They settled into the log cabin that John built in Glen Arbor. He purchased 108 acres of land. Five sons were born to them over the next eight years. John eventually owned his own sloop which he used to carry passengers and freight between Glen Arbor and the town of Frankfort, Michigan.

In 1864, John was drafted into the Union army, joining the Fifteenth Michigan Infantry. Elizabeth kept the farm going while John was away. She had been trained in nursing and midwifery by her own mother and was often called out on emergencies both day and night.

Two more sons were born after John returned home from the war. Elizabeth believed that all of the boys should know how to cook and clean. A reporter for the *Leelanau Enterprise* wrote an article about the Dorseys that focused on Elizabeth. "She trained her seven boys early to do housework. She was the only lady in our part of Leelanau County who, when visitors came, could sit in her parlor and visit with them." The boys were in the kitchen, aprons on, doing the cooking and setting the table for the guests.

John Dorsey passed away in 1903. This cooper's life rolled along as soundly as the barrels he crafted.

46

LENAWEE COUNTY

An Adventurer Takes Up Farming

John Monahan was born in 1830 in the town of Drogheda, County Louth, Ireland. He was the son of John and Margaret Hoy Monahan and the oldest of their three children. John's father was a weaver by trade, just as his own father had been. In the 1800s in Ireland, there were two types of weavers: the rural hand weaver who worked in his own home to supply the needs of his family and neighbors and the more urban weaver who dealt in the larger domestic and export markets. Laws imposed on Irish weavers regulating the export of woolen cloth made it difficult to support their families. When John was seven years old, his father decided to immigrate to America. He landed in New York, where he quickly found work with crews constructing canals and laying rail tracks. He found a place to live and saved nearly all of his money. When he had saved enough for his family's passage to New York, he sent for them. The family joined him in New York, where they lived for two years. In the autumn of 1840, the family traveled to Michigan. They settled in Medina Township in Lenawee County. John Monahan purchased forty acres of uncleared land that he intended to turn to farmland. Young John, now ten years old, helped his father fell trees and clear away scrub brush on their new land. In the wintertime, he was able to attend the local school.

When John reached the age of twenty-five, he was eager for travel and adventure. In 1856, he joined other young men who became mercenaries in the army of William Walker, a man who planned to invade Latin America in order to deal in slaves. Walker, with the tacit approval of President Millard

Fillmore, entered Nicaragua, which was in the midst of a civil war. Walker and his army took control of Nicaragua, whereby Walker then declared himself president. Walker then sent an army to neighboring Costa Rica, but his men were defeated in the Battle of Santa Rosa in March 1856. John Monahan was captured and imprisoned in Grenada. When he was released, John quit Walker's army. He made it to the Isthmus of Panama, where he boarded a steam ship heading for San Francisco. San Francisco's reputation was that of a lawless city. Ever since gold had been discovered in 1848, thousands of adventurers had come into the city. The population swelled to over 200,000. The San Francisco Committee of Vigilance was created with the aim to keep law and order according to its rules. Members patrolled the harbor area, especially watching for new immigrant arrivals, which they did not welcome. John learned to steer clear of the vigilance committee. After three days in the city, he left and made his way to Sacramento. He found work on a ranch owned by two Irishmen named Rooney and Riley. Their spread covered five hundred acres.

One year later, in 1857, John had had enough of the adventurous life. He left California to travel back to Michigan and his father's farm. The next year, John and Elizabeth Haley married. John bought farmland from his father so that he and Elizabeth could set up their own home. Four children were born into the family, but Elizabeth passed away at the age of thirty-eight in 1878. Later that same year, John married again. His second wife was Mary O'Neill. Mary and John brought four more children into the family. As the children grew, John continued expanding his farm holdings. Eventually, his farm grew to encompass 735 acres of land, one of the largest in Lenawee County. He lived the remainder of his life on his farm. His adventurous spirit was laid to rest.

47

LIVINGSTON COUNTY

Escaping Poverty and Memories

The year 1816 was difficult for the poor tenant farmers living in the Barony of Ardee, County Louth, Ireland. The rains fell heavily, and the harvests were poor. People who could not pay their rent were evicted. Around the country, secret societies of mostly Irish Catholic men met to discuss the inequality they saw every day between their lives and the lives of the landlords.

Edward Lynch managed the flax fields owned by an English landlord, William Filgate. He lived with his family in a house on the Filgate property, known as the Wild Goose Lodge because many waterfowl nested in the nearby marshy ground. Edward was sympathetic toward the members of the local agrarian group, the Ribbonmen. He allowed them to meet at his house until their number grew so large he feared retribution from the British authorities. He decided that the society could no longer meet at his house. This decision infuriated the Ribbonmen. One night, they forced their way into the Lynch home. The men flogged Edward and broke the furniture, including his loom used for weaving flax. Eventually, three men were apprehended, brought to trial and given death sentences.

The Ribbonmen vowed revenge on Lynch and his family. On the night of October 16, a group of nearly one hundred men surrounded the Lynch house and set it on fire. In minutes, the house was engulfed in flames. The Ribbonmen stood outside, holding sharp poles should anyone try to escape. When the fire was out, everyone inside was dead. Afterward, suspects were arrested and imprisoned. Eighteen men received death sentences. Some suspects were hanged without having their guilt proven. The memory of that terrible night was spoken about for years. One of the men hanged was named Hugh McCabe.

In that same year, another Hugh McCabe was born to Felix and Rose McCabe, who lived nearby. Hugh and his twin brother, James, were born on May 10, 1816. They had two older brothers, Michael and Patrick. The following year, a sister, Rose Ann, was born. The McCabe children all grew up hearing the story of the tragedy. Eventually, in 1830, Felix and Rose decided the children should immigrate to America. They hoped their children would leave behind memories of the tragedy and find prosperous lives for themselves.

Hugh McCabe was fourteen years old when the five siblings left Ireland. They landed in New York Harbor and then sailed up the Hudson River to Seneca Falls, where they found work. The town boasted sawmills, carding mills, paper mills, cotton mills, distilleries and carriage factories. The McCabes remained in Seneca Falls for a number of years. Hugh met Bridget Monahan from County Sligo, and they married in 1836.

In 1844, Hugh brought his family to Green Oaks Township in Livingston County, Michigan. He purchased eighty acres of land and built a log cabin for his family. Then he began to clear the land for farming. It took three years, but with the help of neighbors and his brother Patrick, who had also bought land in the county, Hugh was able to plant and harvest crops.

In 1861, Bridget McCabe passed away. That same year, when the Civil War started, Hugh's sons Felix, James and Patrick enlisted in the Livingston Volunteers in the Fifth Regiment of the Michigan Infantry. Patrick died soon after from an outbreak of measles. Both Felix and James were captured and imprisoned in Andersonville Prison in Georgia. The camp was notorious for its overcrowding and unsanitary conditions. The water supply was inadequate. Food was scarce. At times, the prison population swelled to four times its capacity. Felix died at Andersonville. James was the only son to survive the war.

Hugh remained on his farm with his other sons, Henry and Hugh. He was popular with his neighbors. When neighbors came to the farm, they called out with a traditional Irish greeting, "Is himself in?" Hugh answered, stating, "Undeniably!" He liked to be known as Hugh "Undeniable" McCabe, or Hughie "Himself" McCabe. When Hugh McCabe died on November 24, 1909, he was buried next to his wife and his already deceased children. Poverty and memories were laid to rest.

48

LUCE COUNTY

In the Land of Opportunity

Joseph Stafford was born in Reading, Berks County, Pennsylvania, on March 28, 1849. He was one of fifteen children born to John and Lydia Stafford. His father, John, had emigrated from Ireland while still a boy. He grew up in southeastern Pennsylvania. When he and Lydia Esselman married, they made their home on a farm John managed. Most of the children continued living near the family home upon reaching adulthood. Only two sons ventured away from Pennsylvania. One of them, Joseph, traveled west to the town of Rossville in Vermillion County, Illinois. He found work as a farmhand and kept at that job during his first year away from home.

The second year in Rossville, Joseph was given a position as a clerk in a drugstore owned by a man named Isaac Warner. Joseph held this job for two years, but then he was ready to move on again. He made his way to Michigan. Joseph relocated in Alcona County, near the town of Harrisville. Like so many others, he was immediately hired on to work in one of the lumber camps. Joseph worked as a lumberman for the next nine years. During this time, Joseph and Mary E. Sayers became acquainted and eventually married. Mary's father had also emigrated from Ireland.

In 1880, Joseph and Mary moved to Otsego County. There was lumber work there as well, but once all of the trees were felled, the company owners pulled out. The lumbermen had to find new camps, moving farther north into the dense forests of northern Michigan. Joseph was able to find work again but only for two years. After that, in 1882, he was elected sheriff of Otsego County.

Lumber camp. *Michigan State University Archives and Historical Collections.*

In 1884, Joseph and Mary came to the Upper Peninsula. In the small town of Newberry, in Luce County, Joseph put his former clerking skills to work for him. He opened a drugstore that became very profitable. Becoming well known in town and well respected, Joseph was asked to serve as the township and village treasurer in Newberry. He accepted these positions and carried out his duties reliably. A few years later, in 1895, Joseph was elected to the board of supervisors for the township, eventually becoming the chairman of the board.

Joseph joined various fraternal and charitable organizations. One of these was the Saladin Temple, Nobles of the Mystic Shrine. The organization originated in New York in 1871. The Nobles of the Mystic Shrine were affiliated with Free Masonry; the founders wanted to create an offshoot of Free Masonry dedicated to fun and fellowship. The organization began attracting many men, who were initiated as members through secret rituals. By the year 1900, there were over fifty-five thousand members who met in Shrine temples throughout the United States. The costumes, headwear and rituals were based on Arabic culture, even though the members were men who followed the beliefs of Christianity. Over the years, the organization's name was shortened to the Shriners. The dominant social work of the organization became the building of hospitals where seriously ill children could be treated without cost.

For a number of years, Joseph suffered from chronic kidney illness known as Bright's Disease, named for the scientist who first associated kidney ailments with cardiovascular diseases. There was no medicine or cure for the disease. Renal failure eventually occurred, causing death. Joseph Stafford was fifty-three years old when Bright's Disease caused his death on December 14, 1902. In his life, he made the most of every opportunity that presented itself to him.

49

MACKINAC COUNTY

The Irish Dragon

Charles O'Malley was born near the town of Newport in County Mayo, Ireland, in the year 1807. As a young man, he considered joining the priesthood of the Catholic Church. He enrolled in the recently established Maynooth College in County Kildare. Charles, however, did not complete his studies. Instead, in 1834, he and his brother Tully set sail for Canada. After their safe arrival, Charles found employment teaching mathematics classes at Laval University, located in the city of Quebec. Neither young man wished to remain in Canada. Instead, they sailed across Lake Huron and landed on Mackinac Island. Here, there was a great deal of commerce going on. The fur trade was thriving. John Jacob Astor was building up a fur trading business that eventually became an empire. Astor hired both Charles and Tully to work for him as clerks.

Within a short time, Charles had made enough money to start his own mercantile business on the island. He opened his shop on the main street of the bustling town. Native Americans, boat captains, sailors, traders, fishermen and other businessmen frequented his store. His business became quite profitable. Charles was regarded as an honest man. People were pleased to do business with him.

Charles had a generous heart where his family and other Irishmen were concerned. He brought his sister, Margaret, and his brothers William and Owen to join him on the island. During the Potato Famine, Charles sent money to bring many starving Irish to America as well. Those who arrived on Mackinac Island or settled on nearby Beaver Island found work as fishermen and exporters of salted fish.

Island House Hotel, Mackinac Island. *Mackinac State Historic Parks Collection.*

In 1846, Charles, or Charlie, as his friends knew him, decided to enter politics. He was elected to the state legislature of Michigan, serving for three years in 1846 and 1847 and again in 1849. He was a man of conviction who spoke his mind. He once quarreled with Henry Schoolcraft. After the quarrel, Charlie saw a way to get back at Schoolcraft for angering him. He created a bill and pushed it through the state legislature, giving himself the right to rename some Michigan counties that already had been named by

Schoolcraft. Charlie chose four Irish county names, and he affixed them to four Michigan counties. He renamed another county to honor the Irish patriot Robert Emmet. The formidable Charlie became known as the "Irish Dragon." In 1850, Charlie was elected justice of the peace on Mackinac Island. He was quick to sentence to prison anyone who provoked him.

In one such instance, Charlie came up against King James Strang of Beaver Island. Ever since Strang and his followers had routed the Irish people and any non-Mormon believers off the island, Charlie harbored an intense dislike of the man. Strang found himself in Judge O'Malley's courtroom after an allegation of physical abuse had been lodged against him. When Strang protested some of Charlie's questions, Judge O'Malley sentenced him to life imprisonment for contempt of court. The charge was later reduced to one year in jail. When Strang was later assassinated, Charlie quickly encouraged the Irish fishermen to return to Beaver Island to reclaim it once again.

Charlie and Tully owned several businesses. They took up lumbering farther north in the state and continued to build on Mackinac Island as well. Charlie had a large hotel built along the Main Street in the town. This became known as the Island House Hotel. The hotel could be seen from the steamships carrying the increasing numbers of visitors to the island. Many people rented rooms in the hotel during their visits. Visitors returned often once the island became a tourist destination.

In 1881, at the age of seventy-four, Charlie O'Malley died. A memorial was placed in St. Anne's Cemetery on Mackinac Island, while his remains were buried across the lake in the town of St. Ignace. The Irish Dragon left his mark on Mackinac Island as well as the state of Michigan.

50

MACOMB COUNTY

A Hero Still Keeps Watch

John Gordon Macomb was born in Belfast, County Antrim, Ireland, in 1717. John Macomb was a prosperous merchant in Belfast, where he traded in luxury goods. In 1755, John decided to immigrate to the British colonies in America. His wife and three children—Alexander, William and Anne—accompanied him. John planned to supply the British colonial forces with the same luxury items he had been selling in Belfast. When England and France went to war in America, the number of British officers in America increased greatly. John's business was based in Albany, New York, the headquarters for the British army. His fine wines, books, snuff and even telescopes were in high demand, making John a very wealthy man.

John's son Alexander was seven years old when the family emigrated. William was four. Alexander remained with the family until he reached the age of eighteen and then made his way to the town of Detroit, Michigan. He began to trade in furs with the local indigenous people. At one time, Alexander's fur business encompassed one-third of the fur trade in North America. Later, William joined him in Detroit. The two brothers were property speculators as well as merchants. They had their base inside the British garrison in the town.

After the American Revolutionary War ended, businessmen who had been sympathetic to the British forces were able to continue doing business without recrimination. The new U.S. government, needing capital, allowed Alexander to buy 4.5 million acres of land in northern New York. The land deal became known as Macomb's Purchase. Alexander, now married with a family, moved everyone to the city of New York. The family occupied a mansion on Broadway, one of the major thoroughfares in the city. Back in Detroit, William continued the family business. By the year 1795, the extended Macomb family owned a great deal of real estate in Detroit, including all of the islands in the Detroit River. The island known as Grosse Ile was the family home.

Alexander Macomb II was born in Detroit on April 3, 1782, before the family moved to New York. His upbringing included a classical education as well as military school. By the time he was sixteen, Alexander II was already a cavalry officer in the New York Rangers. He was one of the first graduates of West Point Academy. When the War of 1812 commenced, Alexander was eager to see action. He took a demotion in rank so that he could join an artillery unit on the front lines.

Alexander was occupied with training new soldiers in upstate New York. His troops were greatly outnumbered by the British forces, 11,500 to 3,500. Alexander's troops were unused to battle. Still, he found a way to defeat the superior British forces. He had his men build a false road, using the terrain at hand and also planting and moving trees. The decoy road led the British forces away from the main battle area into the deep woods where they lost their sense of direction. The diversion gave U.S. naval forces time to win a decisive victory on Lake Champlain. Supplemental troop reinforcements then defeated the British forces. Alexander II became known as the "Hero of Plattsburgh."

After the war, Alexander II returned to Detroit. He continued his army service in Detroit for the next five years. As his military career continued, Alexander II was appointed to positions of increasing authority. In 1828, he was appointed major general and commander-in-chief of the U.S. Army. He held this position for the next thirteen years, until his death in 1841. In addition to the county already named for him, Alexander II had legions of loyal soldiers clamoring for towns, schools and buildings to be named in his honor. He was given the Congressional Medal of Honor by President Madison in 1814. A monument was erected to honor Major General Alexander Macomb II in the city of Detroit in 1908. The Detroit Macomb monument was formed from the melted bronze of cannons seized from the British army during the War of 1812. A man of determination and loyalty still keeps watch over the city of his birth.

51

MANISTEE COUNTY

From Lumberman to Town Leader

Thomas Kenny was born on February 7, 1842, near the market town of Naas, County Kildare, Ireland. He was the son of James and Catherine Dowling Kenny. When Thomas was seven years old, he and his siblings lost both of their parents to typhus in the epidemic of 1849. The children were sent to live with an aunt. Thomas's oldest brother, Edward, left the family to immigrate to America. Edward worked for five years in order to earn enough money to send for his siblings. When the siblings arrived in New York in the autumn of 1854, Edward brought them to Westchester County and then to their new home in Manistee County, Michigan. Edward had been working as a lumberman in Manistee. He knew he could provide for his family there.

A few weeks after the family arrived, Thomas turned thirteen and went to work. He was hired by James O'Neill, who managed a lumber operation. Thomas contracted himself out to other lumber managers for the next sixteen years. Sometimes, he was a log driver on the Manistee River. The job required great strength and concentration. When thousands of logs were floated down the river to the mill, sometimes they jammed, causing the logs behind them to back up for miles. When log drivers saw a jam beginning, they rushed to get to the initial logs caught. They carried peaveys, long poles with a spike on one end. The log driver drove the peavey into a log, then tried to push it out of the way. When there were too many logs caught, dynamite was used to break them apart. The men ran from log to log, balancing precariously as they attempted to get the logs moving. When

Log drive. *Michigan State University Archives and Historical Collections.*

the logs did start moving again, they moved fast. The men had to move faster to avoid being thrown off balance or crushed beneath the heavy load. Many lives were lost during the breaking up of a log jam.

In 1868, when Thomas was twenty-five years old, he and Ellen Lynch decided to marry. Thomas was still working for the lumber companies. He decided, however, that logging was no job for a man who hoped to raise a family. In 1871, Thomas opened a grocery store in the town of Manistee. The store was located on a busy road in the center of the town. The first year, Thomas was in partnership with a man named Charles Grund. The following year, Thomas took on the management of the store by himself.

On the same day as the Great Chicago Fire in 1871, a devastating fire consumed the town of Manistee. The townspeople decided to rebuild, beginning as soon as the embers cooled. They were greatly aided by Thomas Jefferson Ramsdell, the leading attorney in Manistee. He spearheaded the drive to rebuild the town of Manistee in grand style. In only two years, many of the businesses had been rebuilt, and twenty-five new sawmills were in operation.

Thomas saw the aftermath of the fire as an opportunity for him to change direction. In 1879, he returned to lumbering in partnership with a man named Patrick Noud, another emigrant from County Kildare. The partnership was for five years, with the two men taking on a contract with the Manistee Boom Company. They promised to sort and deliver logs to the company in total amount of thirty thousand board feet per year. They delivered on the contract. When the five years were over, they extended the partnership for ten more years. They employed seventy men in their prosperous firm.

Thomas ran for the office of city treasurer of Manistee. He won the election and filled this position from 1875 to 1879. He then became the Manistee County treasurer, serving two terms in 1888 and 1889. When the Manistee Savings Bank was established in 1891, Thomas was elected the first president.

Thomas changed direction again. He opened a coal factory in town, near where Manistee Lake emptied into the Manistee River. He envisioned that coal producing electricity would be essential to the next wave of industry.

Thomas and Ellen raised six daughters, five of whom married locally. Agnes, the youngest, became a woman of business, carrying on her father's spirit of entrepreneurship. Thomas died in 1910, a lumberman and leader nearly his entire life.

52

MARQUETTE COUNTY

The Road to Prosperity

In 1847, Patrick and Mary Nester and their children joined the thousands leaving Ireland. They secured passage on a ship sailing to Canada. The voyage was difficult, but after a few weeks, they arrived safely on the Canadian shore. Patrick was a blacksmith by trade. His skills were in great demand, so finding work was not difficult. The family settled near the town of Kingston. Patrick opened his own blacksmith shop, and Mary took care of the children. On December 25, 1847, Mary gave birth to another son, Timothy.

After three years, Patrick decided that prospects were better for his family across Lake Huron in Michigan. The family moved to Sanilac County. Patrick continued blacksmithing, but he eventually turned away from the trade because the lumber boom was happening all around them and he wanted to be a part of it. Patrick worked as a lumberman until 1864, when he was killed by a falling tree.

Timothy was seventeen when his father passed away. He already knew something about the lumbering business from his father. He made his way to Saginaw, which was a center of lumbering with many sawmills. Timothy found work in one of the lumber camps, remaining in Saginaw for the next eight years. While he was there, he and Mary Sheridan married. Their first child, Hattie, was born in 1870.

In 1872, Timothy and his older brother John contracted themselves with the Michigan Central Railroad to build twenty-five miles of road north of the town of Grayling. Railroad companies were eager to have track laid

Transporting logs. *Michigan State University Archives and Historical Collections.*

throughout the state due to the growth of lumbering and mining industries. Before crews could set down the iron rails, surveyors and engineers determined where a track would be laid down. The road crew prepared and built the roadbed for the track. This could involve digging or blasting through rocks or hills, filling in washes and uneven ground, building trestles and bridges and digging culverts for drainage across streams.

Timothy and John successfully completed their contract. Timothy took out another contract, this time with the Flint & Pere Marquette Railway Company. This contract was for sixteen and a half miles of road. The Flint & Pere Marquette Railway Company owners wanted tracks laid from the town of Flint all the way to the town of Pere Marquette on the Lake Michigan shore. The first twenty miles of the railroad opened on December 1, 1867. From that point westward, the railroad wound its way through the forests of central Michigan. Timothy's contract comprised the final section of the track, and he and his crew finished their section of track on time. In December 1874, the track was completed. There was now a through line from Flint all the way to Lake Michigan.

The lumber industry was moving into Michigan's Upper Peninsula. Timothy, Mary and their two daughters traveled north to Marquette County. Timothy took on lumbering jobs once again. After several years, he had saved enough money to begin buying real estate in the town of Marquette and the surrounding countryside. He became a lumber businessman and a speculator. In 1887, Timothy ran unopposed for the office of mayor of Marquette. Four years later, Timothy and his family, now including a son, Arthur, lived in a beautiful, three-story mansion that had cost nearly $20,000 to build. He built a block of buildings in the center of the town known as the Nester Block. He was one of the original organizers of the Marquette City Street Railway, serving as the organization's first president. He and other investors formed the Munising Railway Company in Alger County, east of Marquette. The road led Timothy Nester to Marquette, where he found prosperity and a place in the history of the county.

53

MASON COUNTY

The Path to the Judiciary

James B. McMahon was born in Washtenaw County, Michigan, to James Sr. and Theodotia McMahon in the year 1848. His father was born in County Down, Ireland, in 1816. James Sr. immigrated to the United States when he was sixteen years old. He found work and saved his money. Two years later, he had saved enough money to travel to the Michigan Territory. Railroad companies were laying tracks in the territory, clearing the way for development. Washtenaw County became a gateway into the Michigan Territory when the Michigan Central Railroad connected some of its towns with Detroit, then farther west. James Sr. bought eighty acres of land that he planned to clear for farming. Following this, he purchased two hundred acres of land in the growing town of Manchester.

Young James worked with his father on the farm. At times, he was able to attend the local log cabin school. He had a keen mind and a deep regard for education. By the age of twelve, he had learned all that he could in the local school. At seventeen years old, James returned to school in the nearby town of Grass Lake. He wanted to seek a college education, but his father was not convinced of the worth of this idea. James continued working on the family farm for another six years.

In 1871, James entered the university located in Ann Arbor. He soon made a name for himself among his fellow classmates. He was the "Prophet" of his sophomore class and an editor of the university newspaper, the *Chronicle*. Four years later, James was selected to give the commencement address.

After graduation, James returned home for five months. In the autumn of 1875, he was hired to work in the law office of C.G. Wing. Wing's law office was in the town of Ludington, over two hundred miles from the family farm. While James was working for Wing, he was also studying to take the bar exam so that he could practice as an attorney. James passed the exam and was admitted to the bar in March 1877. Wing then offered James a partnership in his firm. The two men practiced law together for two years. During this time, James married Emma Stanchfield on March 6, 1878.

In 1881, James was appointed probate judge for Mason County. He held this position for the next four years. He continued practicing law as well as attending to his duties as the probate judge. In 1892, James received a federal appointment: assistant U.S. attorney for the Western District of Michigan. The position required that James and his family move to the town of Grand Rapids. One year later, James received a nomination for the position of circuit judge of the Nineteenth Judicial Circuit of Michigan. His jurisdiction would include the counties of Mason, Manistee, Lake and Osceola. James accepted the nomination and, on Election Day, found himself the winner and the new circuit judge. His official duties began on New Year's Day, 1894. This appointment necessitated Judge McMahon's return to Ludington.

Judge McMahon continued with his duties although he suffered from diabetes and other ailments. He was known as a man of integrity among those he served and his colleagues. In March 1901, James developed pneumonia, which led to his demise on March 15, 1901. His obituary was full of commendations as well as his record of judicial service. Hundreds came to his funeral to hear more accolades bestowed upon James McMahon. Education had started him on the path to the judiciary.

54

MECOSTA COUNTY

Finding and Founding a Village

Dominic O'Brien was born on December 26, 1853, in Newcastle, County Limerick, Ireland. His father passed away when he was nine years old. His mother, Mary Coffee O'Brien, raised her son while managing to remain on the family farm. When Dominic reached the age of fifteen, his mother encouraged him to emigrate, and she helped him secure passage on the British steamship *Manhattan*. Dominic sailed away from his mother and Ireland, landing safely in New York on June 10, 1869. He was able to find work and so remained in New York for the next year.

Dominic heard about the need for lumbermen in the state of Michigan. He decided to head for the town of Saginaw, which was a center for lumbering and shipping as well. Dominic worked as a lumberman for the next four years. He also worked with the crew laying a section of the railroad for the Chicago, Saginaw and Canada Rail Company.

In 1879, when Dominic was twenty-five years old, he boarded the Detroit, Lansing and Northern Railroad, which traveled north to heavily forested areas still untouched by the lumber companies. Dominic got off the train in the newly named village of Mecosta in Mecosta County. With rail transportation, early settlers in the area saw the potential for shipping lumber as well as crops. Those with money of their own or financial backing began to form lumber companies and set up sawmills. Dominic saw at once that what the village would need as it began to grow was a saloon. He anticipated increasing numbers of settlers moving to the area as well as those passing through on their way farther north. He built his saloon, the first wooden frame building, on the main street of the village. Business was very good. One year later, daily train service had been established in the village. More businesses put up buildings on the main street. In 1881, Dominic purchased the newly built Mecosta House Hotel. The hotel building was three stories high with rooms for fifty guests. With the hotel and his saloon/restaurant next door, Dominic was busier than ever and becoming quite prosperous.

Dominic married Maggie Dittell on October 22, 1880. Before his marriage, Dominic had lived in a boardinghouse in the village run by the Estes family. With a family of his own beginning, Dominic bought his own house on a farm. Eventually, he and Maggie welcomed eight children into the family.

Dominic continued to purchase properties and real estate. By 1883, he owned three more buildings in the center of the village as well as two property lots that already had barns constructed on them. His business profits totaled $12,000. The influx of settlers to the area hastened the construction of quite a few businesses and a school, all within the first four years after Dominic arrived in the village. The list of businesses in the village of Mecosta included: wagon shop, general store, livery stable, furniture store, photograph gallery, drugstore, general store, the Wilson House Hotel, dressmaking shop, notions shop, jewelry store, clothing house, bank, shoe shop, clothing store, Mecosta House Hotel, restaurant/saloon, boot and shoe store, saloon, hardware store, meat market, blacksmith, planing mill, grocery, Advance Office, millinery, harness shop, blacksmith, shingles and lumber shop and a barbershop.

There were two physicians in the village and one lawyer. The village even supported its own brass band. Dominic became one of the first trustees of the village council. He lived the remainder of his life in Mecosta, where he died in the year 1912 at fifty-eight. The cause of his death was listed as "exhaustion." When Dominick found himself in Mecosta years earlier, little did he know that he would be remembered as one of its founders.

55

MENOMINEE COUNTY

The Breens of Menominee County

Bartley and Thomas Breen were born in 1834 and 1837, respectively, in Chatham, Northumberland County, New Brunswick, Canada. Their father, Bartholomew Breen, of County Wexford, Ireland, immigrated to Canada in 1813. His father, Daniel Breen, was involved in the Irish Rebellion of 1798. In New Brunswick, Bartholomew worked as a timber cutter for thirty years. He wanted his sons to be educated, so in 1849, he sent Bartley and Thomas to Chicago for schooling. The next year, they were enrolled at St. Mary's College. While they were at college, their father died during an outbreak of cholera. Bartley and Thomas had to leave school.

The Breen family moved to Menominee County in northern Michigan. Elsie Breen was a native of County Limerick, Ireland, and she wanted her family to remain together. Bartley and Thomas found work in a lumber camp. Their brothers, James, David and Michael, joined them as they came of age. Ten years later, all of the Breen brothers were working as lumbermen. David Breen was killed in 1860 after a log jam broke on the Little Cedar River. He was crushed by the moving logs.

When the Civil War began in 1861, Bartley and Thomas volunteered. They enlisted with Company H, Seventeenth Wisconsin Infantry, on December 7, 1861. Their enlistment was for three years or the duration of the war. Bartley Breen was given a commission, which he refused. He wanted to be among the soldiers. The brigade traveled first to Chicago and then to the Shenandoah Valley, where they encountered Confederate forces. Ongoing battles carried the troops through Pennsylvania, West Virginia and Maryland. They fought during the Battle of Gettysburg.

At the sorting grounds. *Michigan State University Archives and Historical Collections.*

Sergeant Bartley Breen was commanded to hold the line at a bridge in Cumberland, Maryland. Confederate forces planned to destroy the railroads and bridges connecting the Union troops with supplies all the way to Ohio. Sergeant Breen requested one man be with him on the bridge. Thomas volunteered. The two brothers stood together, when suddenly, Thomas was struck by two musket balls. The shots entered his face, breaking his nose, and taking the sight from his right eye. Sergeant Breen yelled for men to drag Thomas to cover. He remained at his post. At nightfall, the Confederate forces withdrew without taking the bridge. Sergeant Breen and his men were given a commendation by General Patrick Kelly.

Thomas was carried from the battlefield. The medical doctor who first saw him determined that he was beyond saving, but Thomas was sent to the Reception Hospital in Cumberland. To everyone's surprise, after many months, Thomas recovered. He was discharged and sent home on February 25, 1865. Bartley remained on active duty through the war. He was formally discharged on July 11, 1865.

Back in Menominee, Bartley and Thomas decided to prospect for iron ore in the area of the Menominee River. Their explorations took them sixty miles north, where they found a sizable deposit of iron near the town of Waucedah. The Breen Mine was the first to take iron ore from the Menominee Range. Within fifteen years, there were eight iron mines operating along the Menominee Range. One and a half million tons of iron ore were mined in the first five years.

In addition to mining, Bartley, Thomas and James were timber speculators and timber cruisers. As speculators, they assessed tracts of forested land for the type and quality of the lumber that could be removed. As timber cruisers, they surveyed a plot of land, calculating the amount of board feet of lumber available. The Breen brothers worked independently or contracted with a lumber company.

Bartley married Catherine Jenkins on October 10, 1868. Their family included six daughters, and he became township supervisor. In 1887–88, Bartley was elected to the state legislature. He was nominated for auditor general of Michigan but declined, preferring to remain in Menominee. Thomas served as a justice of the peace. Both men served on the board of trustees for the Catholic Church. Breen Township, located in nearby Dickinson County, was named for the Breens who were so actively involved in the early days of Menominee County.

56

MIDLAND COUNTY

The Forest Makes the Man

John Haley was born on October 24, 1845, in County Wicklow, Ireland. His parents, William and Elizabeth Kehoe Haley, decided that the family must emigrate in order to survive. In 1852, they arrived in Canada and made their new home there. John remained with his parents until he reached the age of nineteen. He left Canada as wintertime was approaching and arrived in Tuscola County, where logging operations were commencing. John found work in one of the lumber camps, and the following winter, he worked in another camp in Midland County. A few years later, on January 18, 1870, John and Mary Keeley married in Saginaw, Michigan. John and Mary planned to make their home in the town of Midland. John went to work for John Larkin, one of the biggest lumber company owners in Midland. He took over the management of Larkin's lumber interests. John stayed in Larkin's employ for nine years. During this time, three children were born into the family. John's parents came to live in Midland so they could be close to the family.

Around 1880, John decided to branch out, offering his lumbering expertise independently. In 1883, he joined with G.W. Covert to form their own business in lumbering. During the winter of this year, the firm procured a vast amount of board feet of lumber from two hundred acres of land they owned. This property was known as the Eastman farm, a prime piece of land known throughout the county. They had 125 lumbermen at a time in the woods, working in teams of 6–7 men each. Their saws chopped through the old-growth trees in record time and numbers.

Sawmill, Midland. *Michigan State University Archives and Historical Collections.*

In town, John went into business with R.W. Clason. Their firm of Clason and Haley dealt in the livery and undertaking business. They owned their own stables where they kept twenty horses and the equipment needed for their livery services. They built coffins and transported the deceased to the cemetery for burial.

John Haley owned 120 acres of land in Larkin Township. Another son, John, was born into the family in 1884. The Haley family was well known in the county. John was serving on the Larkin Village board when he accepted the appointment of village supervisor. The forest formed the man he became, industrious and honest, a man with many lifelong friends. He passed away in March 1911. He was laid to rest beneath the trees in Old Calvary Catholic Cemetery in Midland.

57

MISSAUKEE COUNTY

Wandering Til You Find Home

The son of a schoolteacher from Ireland, James Cavanaugh was born on September 25, 1847. His father, Daniel, immigrated to Canada while still a young man. He took up farming in Quebec, where he resided for a few years. He then moved around from Vermont to New York and then back to Canada. He and Elizabeth Harrison, another Irish immigrant, married and raised a family of twelve children. James was born in Haldimand County, in the province of Ontario.

When James was sixteen years old, he left the family farm. He found work about forty miles west of London, Ontario, where men were drilling for oil. James stayed with the job for one year. Like his father, James had no reservations about moving on to a new place to see what opportunities might await him. He crossed Lake Huron into Michigan and found work in a lumber camp. The boat anchored in Bay City, from which lumber and all kinds of other goods were shipped.

After one year, James tired of the life of a lumberjack and returned to the family home. He stayed for a year and then left for Illinois. He worked as a farm laborer, but that was not to his liking either. Back in Michigan, he found work in a sawmill in Bay County. As he was careful with his earnings, he saved $400 in one year.

Now twenty-two years old, James used his money to buy land in Missaukee County. It took him many years to clear ninety acres of the land. He built a home on the property, and in 1879, he and Emma Stout

38 "Peelika-polika"
Italians peeling cedar posts
at Au Sable.

Peeling cedar logs. *Michigan State University Archives and Historical Collections.*

married. The homestead and farm sustained them. They lived there with their children until 1892.

In 1892, James moved his family into the town of Lake City. He took charge of a store frequented by the members of the local Patrons of Industry chapter. The Patrons of Industry was a nonpartisan farmers' organization. The founder was a religious minister, F.W. Vertican, who noticed that most of his congregants felt powerless to improve aspects of their lives. He wanted people to use their collective voices to advocate for better working conditions and prices for crops. The organization initially had thousands of members, but as conditions improved for farmers, membership dropped. James resigned from the store in order to accept a new position.

James's new employment was cashier of the Missaukee County Bank, located in Lake City. The position elevated James into some prominence in the county. He found himself a favored candidate for elected civic and political positions. At various times, he was the constable and the township supervisor and the superintendent of the poor for five years. James decided whether or not a destitute person's situation merited financial assistance from the county. If not, he directed the person to the poorhouse.

James Cavanaugh continued as the bank cashier well into the new century. At home, three more sons were born into the family. Eventually, James became a loan officer with the bank, a position he held throughout the remainder of his working years. He passed away on February 2, 1922, at the age of seventy-four. James left his wandering days behind him once he found his home in Missaukee County.

58

MONROE COUNTY

Shepherding His Flock

Eugene Downey, of County Cork, and Abbie White, of County Kerry, Ireland, married and immigrated to Canada, settling near Toronto. They established a home, and Eugene took up farming. Eugene became well known and respected in the community. To honor the Downey family, the town of Downeyville was named for them. After some years, the family moved to Cass County, Michigan. They came to live in the township of Silver Creek, where they raised their family. Eighteen children were born to them, and they were devout Catholics. Their son James was born on January 23, 1873. James felt that he had a calling to the priesthood, so when he had completed his education in the local school, he left the family farm. He was accepted into Notre Dame in South Bend, Indiana.

After his years at Notre Dame, James continued his education in Assumption College in Sandwich, Ontario. He graduated with a degree in philosophy in 1898. James then entered Mount St. Mary's Seminary, located in Cincinnati, Ohio. He completed his theological studies and was ordained on July 7, 1901, by the bishop of Detroit, Reverend John S. Foley. Two months later, the Reverend Father Downey received his first assignment. He was sent to St. Mary of the Immaculate Conception Church in Monroe, Michigan. St. Mary's Church was established in 1788. Its original name was St. Antoine of Padua, bestowed upon it by the French Catholics who had come to the area from Quebec. The name was changed to St. Mary of the Immaculate Conception in 1845. At St. Mary's, Father Downey served as an assistant to the pastor, Father Joseph Joos. His duties included offering Masses; visiting the sick; conducting baptisms, weddings and funerals; encouraging parents to support the parochial school; and comforting parishioners during hard times. The parish continued to grow. St. Mary's School had an enrollment of nearly 350 students, and 400 attended Sunday School classes. Father Downey soon became a popular figure at St. Mary's. He had an easygoing manner and a tireless spirit.

Father Downey remained at St. Mary's until 1913. During his time in Monroe, Father Downey had shown a strong civic mindedness as well. When election days came around, he did not favor one candidate over another along party lines. Instead, he supported whichever candidate he felt would do the most good for the people. This attitude endeared him to everyone, not just those who were affiliated with the Catholic Church or St. Mary's Parish. He enjoyed the high regard of business leaders and local government officials.

In 1913, Father Downey was transferred to Immaculate Conception Parish in Anchorville, Michigan, in St. Clair County. Anchorville was originally called Au Lac (near the lake) by the early French explorers who founded the town in the late 1700s. The church was built and dedicated in 1853. Father Downey took to his new home as easily as he had to the parish in Monroe, and he remained the pastor of Immaculate Conception for twenty-two years. When fire swept through the parish complex on August 26, 1917, Father Downey first consoled his parishioners and then told them they would rebuild. One year later, a new church and school were completed.

Everyone who knew Father Downey spoke of his compassion for people. As the years went on, he was beleaguered with health problems stemming from the onset of diabetes and heart disease. Even when he was not feeling well, Father Downey faithfully administered to his parishioners. He died suddenly on September 18, 1935. His funeral Mass was celebrated as a High Requiem Mass, and over 1,000 people attended the service. Prominent leaders of the Catholic Diocese attended, including 4 monsignors, 110 fellow priests and 50 religious sisters. Father Downey's parishioners honored him with moving tributes recalling how he shepherded his flock.

59

MONTCALM COUNTY

The Business of Making Cheese

John M. Fitzpatrick lived over thirty years of his life in Sardinia, New York, before he came to Montcalm County, Michigan. His father, Thomas Fitzpatrick, born in 1815, was a native of County Clare, Ireland. When Thomas emigrated, his new home was in Springville, New York. His future wife, Mary Cottrell, was a native of Utica, New York. Thomas was a farmer and a blacksmith. In 1859, Thomas and Mary moved their family to the town of Sardinia, in Erie County, New York. Their son John was born on September 17, 1856, eventually one of thirteen children. Eleven of the children lived long lives into adulthood, an uncommon experience in the nineteenth century.

On the family farm, John's mother taught him how to make cheese. Like other immigrant mothers, she brought the knowledge of making cheese with her when the family crossed the ocean to America. As the population rose in East Coast cities, men who knew how to make cheese began buying the extra milk farmers brought to them. After the American Revolution, New York State became the top producer of cheeses, which were then shipped up and down the East Coast. When the Erie Canal was completed, implements and supplies for making cheese were easier to come by. Large-scale cheese production spread to the Ohio Valley and Wisconsin.

In 1880, John and Luella Hopkins married. Three daughters were born during the next eight years. The family continued to reside in Sardinia, but John was eager to relocate in Michigan. The family arrived in the village of Butternut in Montcalm County in 1890. John had heard of two men starting up a cheese factory in Butternut. He was hired to work at their company known as Cross and Isham. The following year, John purchased Isham's half of the partnership. The first years for the factory were difficult. Butternut was only a small village, and there were only five or six farmers who brought their milk to the factory. John and Mr. Cross decided that they would sell their cheese in nearby Stanton, a larger town. There was a cheese factory in Stanton, but over time, the men were able to build up their business. Eventually, John bought out Cross's share of the business.

John's brother Henry had also located in Montcalm County. He resided in the village of Carson City, only a few miles south of Butternut. In 1894, the two brothers decided to open a cheese factory in Carson City. They bought a creamery already in operation and then modified it to become their cheese factory. The factory proved successful. John sold his share of the business to Henry and then formed a new partnership with a man named Chauncey Case. John and Chauncey opened a cheese factory in the nearby town of Fenwick. When that business was running successfully, John opened another cheese factory in the town of Crystal. He was managing all three factories by the year 1900.

At the height of production, the factories were taking in 20,000 pounds of milk per day. The Annual Report of the Michigan Dairyman's Association showed that for the year 1904, the factory in Butternut took in over 3 million pounds of milk, which converted to 316,356 pounds of cheese produced.

Eventually, John Fitzpatrick concluded the business of making cheese and sold his factories. He wanted to devote time to his own farm of 120 acres. He and his family still resided in the town of Butternut. He was not active politically, but he took an interest and lent his support to endeavors that increased the prosperity of the town and its residents. He passed away on November 26, 1922.

60

MONTMORENCY COUNTY

Life in the Poorhouse

Some Irish immigrants found prosperity in their adopted country, but others did not fare as well. In the mid to late nineteenth century, poorhouses were built to accommodate people who were considered indigent or feeble or morally "fallen." There were two kinds of relief people who had fallen on hard times could seek: outdoor relief, which allowed a person to remain at home with some assistance, or indoor relief. People sent to the poorhouse received indoor relief. Poorhouses were funded through taxes paid by residents of a locality, so most taxpayers wanted only "the deserving poor" to receive help. The town overseer of the poor determined whether someone was deserving. Children who had lost their parents presented an obvious need for help. Until orphanages were built, children were often sent to the poorhouse if there was no one to take them in. Unmarried pregnant women, considered morally degraded, were often sent to the poorhouse. Elderly or sick people could be sent to the poorhouse. Physically disabled people or those deemed mentally unfit were sent to the poorhouse.

Two ideas that led to the institution of poorhouses were the divine hand of God punishing those who were not worthy of prosperity and the notion that people who had to beg for aid were inherently lazy and had dispositions inclined to become overly dependent on others. Reformers of the time believed the poorhouse should be a place where inhabitants were reformed and rehabilitated. Living in the poorhouse was meant to be a temporary situation.

To encourage rehabilitation, poorhouse residents worked on the poor farm. They worked in the fields and garden to help defray the cost of their care. Women worked in the kitchen preparing meals. Children might be hired out as servants in houses. There was a paid manager who oversaw the running of the poor farm. The manager was usually assisted by a matron, often his wife, who saw to the daily needs of the residents. Since the poorhouse and the poor farm were funded by the local government, officials wanted to keep costs down. Often, this resulted in the residents doing without basic necessities of daily living. There were rarely inspections or regulations pertaining to the running of the poorhouse or poor farm. People feared being sent to either place.

Eventually, inspections and regulations were put in place for poorhouses. One result of the inspections was the decision to remove children from the premises. This led to the first orphanages being built. Dorothea Dix, a socially conscious reformer, led the way for having separate institutions built for people suffering from mental health disorders in America. Criminals were removed from the poorhouse and incarcerated in separate buildings.

In 1830, the Michigan Territorial Legislature enacted a law requiring every county to have a poorhouse. Montmorency County, organized in 1840, had its poorhouse in the town of Atlanta. One Irish immigrant's son's story ended there.

George Faught was the son of Lawrence and Bridget Fogarty Faught. Bridget was an Irish immigrant, and George was born in 1837 in New York, the youngest of three children. The family came to Sanilac County, Michigan, where, by 1860, Bridget and her three children were on their own due to Lawrence's death. Both George and his older brother, William, took up farming and lumbering for the next several years. George married Elizabeth Miller in 1867. Elizabeth was not well and did not live to see their only child, a daughter, born in 1870, grow up. George put his daughter into the care of his wife's parents while he continued farming in Sanilac County. His daughter married when she was nineteen years old, and she and her husband moved to Montmorency County. Eight children were born into the family. George found his way to Montmorency County in his later years, though he was not in good health. George wanted to live near his daughter, but at sixty-five years old, he could not live on his own, nor could he earn a living. Thus, George Faught sought admission into the county poorhouse, where he remained for 114 days until his death in 1905.

61

MUSKEGON COUNTY

To Serve Those in Need

Alfred Allen was born in the city of Cork, in County Cork, Ireland, on May 1, 1849. His father, Benjamin Allen, was born in Belfast in 1816. He was the prosperous owner of three paper mills that employed more than eight hundred people. Benjamin carried on the largest trade in paper in the country. He was a fair employer who concerned himself with his employees' welfare. Alfred's mother, Patience Humphries Allen, was the daughter of Professor John Dobbs Humphries, a noted lecturer and poet at Queen's College Cork. There were sixteen children in the family, although several died in infancy. The family were Quakers, also known as the Religious Society of Friends.

When the potato crop in Ireland was ruined for a second year in 1846, the Quakers realized that a terrible crisis was at hand. A committee met in Dublin to formulate a plan of assistance for the starving people. Society members in England sent donations of money and clothing to relief centers in Ireland. The society opened soup kitchens where they fed thousands of people every day. There were Quaker soup kitchens in the cities of Cork, Waterford, Limerick, Tipperary and Wexford.

Benjamin Allen did what he could to help the people in Cork. He traveled throughout the parish in his carriage, searching for people in dire need. He collected these people and brought them home to his estate, where he housed them in cottages on his property and cared for them personally.

In 1860, a free-trade law went into effect in Ireland. This law removed any tax on the importation of paper from other countries. One effect of the law was the ruination of Benjamin Allen. His business could not compete with the less expensive paper coming into the country. His financial empire was bankrupt, and all of his paper mills closed.

Alfred was eleven when his father's business collapsed. He had been attending the Quaker School in the city. At age fourteen, Alfred left school. He found employment in a pharmaceutical house owned by John Hatton. Alfred learned the business of manufacturing drugs, compounding mixtures, preparing medicines and salesmanship. He remained with Hatton for five years, until poor health incapacitated him. Alfred was advised to seek a drier, warmer climate, so he traveled to Madrid, Spain. He was hired by a Baptist missionary, Professor Knapp, to sell Bibles. Alfred came to know Caroline Tisdall, an English governess working for a prominent family. Alfred and Caroline decided to marry. They traveled to London and were married on August 31, 1871. Following the wedding, Alfred and Caroline boarded a ship that carried them to the United States.

When they arrived in New York City, Alfred and Caroline traveled on to Michigan. They came to the town of Olivet, in Eaton County, where Alfred was hired to work in the local drugstore. Shortly thereafter, Alfred found another position as a druggist in Portland, Michigan. The drugstore was owned by W.W. Bogue. Alfred worked for Bogue for seven years, eventually managing the Portland store and another store in Sunfield, where he and Caroline lived. Alfred traveled between the two stores every day. Soon Caroline gave birth to the first of their ten children.

In 1878, Alfred moved his family to the town of Montague, in northern Muskegon County. He worked as a pharmacist in C.L. Brundage's store for seven years. For seven more years, Alfred worked in L.G. Ripley's store, also in Montague. After twenty-one years, Alfred was ready to open his own drugstore.

Alfred Allen opened his store in Montague in 1893 and operated the store for four years before ill health forced him to retire. Alfred had carried on the legacy of serving others he learned from his father. The medicines and healing ointments he had prepared throughout his working years brought relief to many people. Alfred passed away at age forty-eight on November 4, 1897.

62

NEWAYGO COUNTY

The Grand Old Man of Newaygo County

James Barton was born on June 4, 1812, in County Tyrone, Ireland. He was the second son born to William and Susannah Culton Barton. In 1824, William, Susannah and their sons boarded the ship *Providence* and sailed for Quebec. When the family stepped off the boat, Susannah died from the acute gastritis she had endured during the crossing. William and the boys did not linger. They headed for Lyons Township in Wayne County, New York, where William bought a farm.

When James was seventeen years old, in 1829, the family moved to Bloomfield Township in Oakland County, Michigan. James had attended school in Ireland and in New York, and so, in 1831, James began teaching in the local school. The following year, he and Reliance Jenne married on March 25, 1832. Reliance was sixteen. Her parents, Lettes and Fear Swift Jenne, both passed away before she was twelve years old. One year later, Charles Barton was born.

In August 1833, James, Reliance and baby Charles came to the village of White Pigeon, located in St. Joseph County. After two years, they moved to the village of Thornton in Cook County, Illinois, where James took up farming. For four years, James was a justice of the peace. In 1845, the family settled on a farm in Berlin Township, Ionia County, Michigan, with James accepting a request to be the township supervisor. The next year, James bought another farm in nearby Otisco Township. The family lived there until the winter of 1850. There were now five more children in the family.

James arrived in Newaygo County early in 1850, prospecting for land to buy. His brother, William, had previously arrived, purchasing six hundred acres of prairie land. James purchased two hundred acres near William's section in Big Prairie Township. There were no roads or even rough tracks. In order to get to their new land, the family loaded all of their belongings on a raft and floated everything across the Muskegon River. James wasted no time. He and his sons had all two hundred acres in use that same year.

James began studying the law, and in 1852, was elected a county judge. That same year he was nominated to represent his district in the state legislature. James headed to the state capitol in Lansing, but when he arrived, he found that King James Strang, the Mormon leader from Beaver Island, already occupied the legislative seat. Neither man had been aware of the other man's candidacy. Beaver Island and Newaygo County were part of the same legislative district. When the votes were counted again, Strang came out the winner, so James returned to Newaygo. He remained a county judge through 1853. He was then elected probate judge and served six years. In 1858, James was admitted to the bar and became the first prosecuting attorney of the county, serving five years. In 1870, he was appointed probate judge by Governor Henry P. Baldwin and served until his retirement. He was also circuit court judge for six years and a township supervisor for over thirty years. James Barton served in some official capacity in Newaygo County for more than forty years.

Eventually, James's son Henry bought three hundred acres of land near his father's property. He already owned five hundred acres of pine forest. Another son, George, managed the family farm. Reliance passed away in 1886 at the age of seventy. James married Catherine Neville the following year. She passed away in 1892. He then married Polly Herrington in 1894. James practiced law for thirty-seven years from his office in the town of Newaygo. He rode into town from his farm fourteen miles away every Monday morning, remaining until Saturday evening. He continued this routine until he was eighty-three years old. James Barton passed away at the age of ninety-two on February 16, 1905. He had come to be known as the Grand Old Man of Newaygo County. James said of himself, "I am but only a humble follower of the plow."

63

OAKLAND COUNTY

It's All About the Land

Peter Fagan was fifteen years old when he emigrated from Ireland with his parents and two brothers, Thomas and John. He was born on August 23, 1808, in Drogheda, County Louth. His parents were Terrence and Bridget Fagan. The family arrived in New York in 1823, settling near the town of Albany, where construction of the Erie Canal, connecting the Hudson River with Lake Erie, offered steady work. Peter found work with a crew of blasters, setting off canisters filled with gunpowder in order to open up solid limestone rock along the canal route. After the Erie Canal was finished, Peter worked on the railroad, also heading west. The Fagan family remained in New York for nine years.

In 1832, when Peter was twenty-four and John was twenty-one, they left New York to prospect in the Michigan Territory. They joined a gang building a military road that became known as the Detroit and Saginaw Turnpike. Construction halted when wintertime settled in, so the brothers returned to New York. The following spring, Peter and John convinced their parents and brother, Thomas, to relocate to Michigan with them. The family came to Holly Township in Oakland County. The new turnpike passed through the center of the township, leading the Fagans to surmise that the township would soon grow, even though at the time of their arrival, the land was densely covered in oak and hickory forests.

The Fagans were the third family to settle in the township. The brothers and their father bought land at $1.25 per acre in four of the township's thirty-six sections. Everyone worked to clear the land so that it could be turned to farming. When Peter's land was cleared, he sold his section so that he could buy four more uncleared sections. Peter built a rough shanty for himself and kept "bachelor's hall." The little cabin was ten feet square and just over six feet high. There was a massive fireplace on one end, two windows on one side and a window and a door across the floor on the other side. The remaining wall had a bed against it, as well as a flour barrel and a pork barrel.

Peter and Eliza Laura Dains married on December 16, 1838, the first wedding performed in Holly Township. After the service, Peter and Eliza loaded their wagon, pulled by oxen, and started for their new home. Eliza was seventeen years old, the daughter of Stephen Dains, who had also come from New York. Eliza, upon seeing the shanty, said that "she could live in it for a time if he could." Six months later, Peter had finished building a larger log cabin, and they moved into their new home.

In 1841, the first of Peter and Eliza's twelve children was born. Eventually, Peter needed to build a larger frame house to accommodate his growing family. The new house was ready in 1853. Peter came to be well known in the community. He became the highway commissioner and the township assessor. He was seen as a man of "such excellent business qualifications and sound judgment." Later, Peter became the township supervisor, township clerk and drain commissioner. When the township was granted a post office, Peter selected its name, Holly Mills. A history of Oakland County records that his reputation was that of a "careful and industrious farmer" who with "patient toil, together with a rigid practice of economy, and a faculty for making everything go its utmost extent," earned the success of his labors.

In time, Terrence and Bridget Fagan passed away. John and Thomas Fagan farmed alongside each other and shared a home. When they had not been seen for some days, neighbors went to investigate. Both men were dead inside their home. Thomas was seventy-eight years old and John eighty-two. Peter died in the same year as his brothers on March 18, 1893. Over the years, he had divided his land among his children so that each of them owned land of their own. Eliza passed away ten years later after living for seventy-two years in the same home on the same land. Truly, it is all about the land.

64

OCEANA COUNTY

The Women Next To, Not Behind, the Men

Maria Goldie was born in County Longford, Ireland, on March 10, 1816. When she was ten years old, her family moved to Glasgow, Scotland. At the age of fifteen, she and John Haughey were married. Their son, William, was born the following year. The family left Glasgow and moved to London. In 1848, Maria, John and William sailed to America. After landing in New York, they made their way to Memphis, Tennessee. They had only been in Memphis for a short while when John passed away. The following year, Maria and William moved to Milwaukee, Wisconsin. In 1852, Maria married again. Her second husband was James O'Hanlon, another Irish emigrant from Lurgan, County Armagh, Ireland. James had been living in Claybanks Township in Oceana County, Michigan, since 1849. Maria and William returned with James to Claybanks.

While James became well known among the other early settlers by holding various township offices, Maria had the honor of owning the first cow brought into the county. She was also the first schoolteacher in the township. Eventually, the township of Goldie was named for her.

Maria's son, William, was twenty years old when he moved with his mother and stepfather to Claybanks. He helped to clear James's land for farming. William had acquired peach pits from growers on the East Coast, and he planted these in the newly plowed fields, where they grew very well. Maria sold peaches from these early trees for twenty-five cents each since they were quite a delicacy. The following year, William planted flower and apple seeds, which also did well.

Catherine Anna Clark met William Haughey in 1855 when he was visiting the city of St. Louis, Missouri, where she lived. Catherine was born in County Longford, Ireland, in 1835. She was six years old when she immigrated with her parents, Patrick and Mary Clark, to the United States. They lived in Schuylkill County, Pennsylvania, for nine years and then moved to St. Louis. Both parents succumbed during an outbreak of cholera in the city. William and Catherine married in St. Louis on April 19, 1855. Afterward, William took Catherine to Claybanks to meet his mother.

Maria encouraged William and Catherine to settle in Claybanks. William bought land and began to build a house. He and Catherine cleared two acres of land by hand, as they did not own a team of oxen or horses. Catherine did not shy away from the hard work. She piled scrub brush, dug stumps from the ground and rolled logs. When the ground was ready, William planted corn, potatoes, squash, carrots, peas, beans and his peach trees, apple trees and flowers. He was eager to try planting any seed crops he could get his hands on. During this same time, they welcomed their firstborn child, a daughter, who was soon followed by two sons. All in all, seven children came into their family.

William served for ten days in the Union army in 1863. He then paid a substitute to take his place and returned home. He built a sawmill and shingle mill. William also opened a retail store. In later years, he added a meat market and grocery store as well. In 1871, the mill burned down, but William rebuilt it. He sold it two years later to E.D. Richmond and Company.

The family moved to the town of Pentwater, where Catherine and William took over the management of the Sherman House Hotel. On the night of April 23, 1875, the hotel and the nearby Methodist Episcopal church were consumed by fire. William reported that he had "lost everything but his grit." A few years later, William's stepfather and his mother passed away. William opened a store, but that, too, burned to the ground. Catherine and William left Pentwater to live in Shelby Township.

In 1900, William continued storekeeping with Catherine's help. Their son William lived with them; he was a druggist in town. William Sr. passed away the following year on September 11, 1901, at the age of sixty-eight years. Catherine stood next to William in every endeavor they undertook, an essential partner in their success. She passed away on May 7, 1917.

65

OGEMAW COUNTY

It Happened in Ogemaw County

Thomas Harper was the son of an Irish immigrant mother and English immigrant father. He was born on September 7, 1852, in North Perth County, Canada. Thomas grew up on the family farm and became a farmer as well. In 1885, Thomas and Fannie Terry married. She was the daughter of Zacheriah and Eliza Terry. Thomas and Fannie moved to Michigan the following year. They settled near the town of West Branch in Ogemaw County, where Thomas bought land for a farm. They became the parents of six children.

In 1897, Thomas was appointed superintendent of the poor farm of Ogemaw County. He was supervisor for the next fifteen years. One year after Thomas became the superintendent, an extraordinary event occurred in Ogemaw County. Thomas and his family were caught up in the excitement, as was everyone else in the county and the entire state.

The year 1898 was an election year in Ogemaw County. Most of the residents were members of the Republican Party. Three weeks before Election Day, Merrie Hoover Abbott was put forth by the Democratic Party for the seat of prosecuting attorney. Merrie Hoover was born in St. Johns, Michigan, in 1873. She was working as a stenographer for the Marshall Field & Company in Chicago when she met Charles Abbott. They married in 1894 and went to live in West Branch, where they opened a mercantile store.

Merrie convinced Charles that they should both attend law school, so they enrolled at the University of Michigan in Ann Arbor. Charles graduated in 1897; Merrie obtained her degree in 1898. They returned to West Branch intending to practice law. The townspeople thought it very unusual for a woman to be an attorney. Furthermore, Merrie aligned herself with the Democrats.

During the 1890s, some Democrats, calling themselves the Silverites, advocated for the return of the silver standard. Silver was plentiful and used by farmers and laborers. The government had switched to a gold standard in 1873, which favored wealthy businessmen. The gold standard made it more difficult for farmers and laborers to borrow money, repay loans or receive credit. Merrie Abbott stood with the Silverites.

Word spread that Merrie's name was on the ballot. People laughed, but Merrie believed that she could win. She campaigned vigorously for the Democratic Union Free Silver Party and its policies and added thoughts of her own. She was an accomplished speaker, using her wit and convictions to gain supporters.

On Election Day, the men eligible to vote went to the polls. After counting, the two candidates were tied. There was an immediate recount, and this time, Merrie won by four votes. The news spread throughout the country—even the *New York Tribune* picked up the story. Merrie's opponent, incumbent William T. Yeo, refused to relinquish his position. Merrie threatened to put him in the county jail. The current state attorney general, Fred A. Maynard, stated that Merrie could not take office without a ruling by the Supreme Court. The incoming state attorney general, Horace Oren, filed an application to have Merrie removed from office.

The case came before the Supreme Court in June 1899; Merrie spoke on her own behalf. She stated that since she had graduated from law school, had been admitted to the bar, was nominated for the office of prosecuting attorney and "received the votes necessary for her election," it followed that she was the rightful and legal person to hold the office. She had two advocates, Circuit Court Judges Allen B. Morse and Thomas A.E. Weadock, from Detroit, who spoke in support of her.

Horace Oren argued since a woman could not vote, she could not hold office. After the hearing, Merrie Abbott returned to West Branch. The court ruled against Merrie, and she was removed from office. She had been the Ogemaw County prosecuting attorney for ten months. She had tried 156 cases, losing only one.

Merrie and Charles Abbott moved to Detroit. In 1936, Emelia Schaub was hailed as the first female prosecutor in Michigan. A news reporter went to see Merrie, who humbly recalled what happened in Ogemaw County thirty-eight years earlier. Merrie Hoover Abbott passed away in October 1946. Her pioneering spirit was of the mind.

66

ONTONAGON COUNTY

Copper!

In the mid-seventeenth century, indigenous people took French missionaries to see a massive boulder of copper inland from the Ontonagon River. Years later, in 1766, a fur trader from Mackinac Island, Alexander Henry, traveled down the Ontonagon River in order to glimpse this wonder of nature. He described it to investors from England in 1771. They were interested in mining the copper, so they sent Henry back to the area to set up mining facilities. The riverbank collapsed on top of the first mines dug so Henry had to give up. The area was left unsettled and unmined for the next seventy years.

In 1841, the Ontonagon Boulder, as it was called, came to the attention of a man from Detroit named Julius Eldred. He wanted to acquire the boulder and then exhibit it in the cities back east. Julius was granted a trading permit to acquire the rock. He went to Ontonagon along with an interpreter who assisted him in negotiations with the local indigenous people. Julius agreed to pay the tribe $150 for the rock: $45 immediately and the remainder in goods distributed over the next two years.

Secretary for War James M. Porter ordered General Walter Cunningham, the U.S. mineral agent in the area, to seize possession of the boulder from Julius for the U.S. government. The Ontonagon Boulder was transported to Washington, D.C., where it was displayed in the National Museum of Science at the Smithsonian Institution.

In 1843, the government opened a mineral land office in the Upper Peninsula for mining purposes. A miner named Christopher Columbus

Copper miners loading tram cars. *Michigan Technological University Archives and Copper Country Historical Collections.*

Cushin attempted to once again start copper mining along the Ontonagon River. He moved downstream from Alexander Henry's former site and began his operation in 1849. One year later, the Forest Company took over the Cushin Mine site, which became a successful copper mine. In 1852, the Glenn Mining Company was formed from the Forest Company. Six years later, the Glenn Mining Company was reorganized into the Victoria Copper Mining Company. This was the beginning of the copper boom in Michigan.

James Flannigan, a miner, was born in 1814 or 1816 in County Waterford, Ireland. After he immigrated to the United States, James heard about the mineral resources in Michigan's Upper Peninsula. James arrived in Ontonagon County in 1848 and found work in the Forest Company Mine. When he had saved enough money, James sent for his wife, Ellen, and their children. They arrived safely and settled into the town that grew up around the Victoria Mine. When his son Thomas reached the age of twenty-one, he, too, became a copper miner.

Ten children were born into the family over the next twenty years. James worked as a mine captain until 1868; at fifty-two years old, he longer had the physical stamina required of a miner. He and Ellen and the six children at home moved to the town of Marquette, Michigan. Two years later, there

Copper miners underground with candle lamps. *Michigan Technological University Archives and Copper Country Historical Collections.*

Miners laying rail tracks in a copper mine. *Michigan Technological University Archives and Copper Country Historical Collections.*

was an economic slump that caused the price of copper to drop disastrously. Copper companies folded, leaving hundreds unemployed. The Victoria Mine, from which more than two hundred tons of copper had been taken, was mostly idle.

In Marquette, James went to work as a watchman for the railroad. His oldest son, Thomas, worked as a railroad engineer. His son Richard, who was eleven years old, continued his education and eventually was admitted to the bar and practiced law. He became a justice of the peace in the town of Norway. James moved to Norway in his later years, where he passed away on March 3, 1891, at seventy-five. James was there when copper was king.

67

OSCEOLA COUNTY

Provider for the Family

William Horner, born in St. Catharines, Ontario, Canada, was the oldest son of Samuel and Elizabeth Walker Horner. Samuel Horner was born in 1817 in the Irish province of Ulster. His ancestors were French Huguenots, Protestants who fled France in the late 1600s when King Louis XIV imposed Catholicism as the state religion. Samuel emigrated from Ireland at a young age. He became a schoolteacher, both in Canada and in upper New York State, for more than twenty years. Elizabeth Walker, also an Irish immigrant, met and married Samuel. Their son William was born on August 23, 1851.

Samuel Horner passed away in 1862 at the age of forty-five. Eleven-year-old William was now the head of the house and the sole provider for his mother and four younger siblings. The family relocated to Baltimore, Maryland, where William took a job as a telegraph messenger and operator. He kept at that job until he reached the age of fifteen. William and his mother then moved the family back to Canada, this time settling in Stratford, Ontario. William found a position as an assistant in a general mercantile shop, and he remained in the shop for the next four years. His next employment was that of a bookkeeper with the Scrimgeour Brothers, general contractors and builders, in Stratford. William worked for that company for six years. During his time with the company, William and Margaret Pullar of Stratford married on December 30, 1874. Two years later, their first son, Samuel, was born.

By now, the year was 1877. William was nearly twenty-six years old. His younger siblings could provide for themselves. William, Margaret "Maggie" and Samuel moved to Deseronto, Ontario. William took a position with H.B. Rathbun & Son, a general contracting and shipbuilding firm. He became a contractor in the manufacturing department and had twenty men working under him. Another child was born into the family during William's three years with the firm.

In 1880, William removed his family from Stratford. They moved into Warren County, Pennsylvania, where William took on a position with L.D. Wetmore & Company. William was the superintendent of the business, which sold doors, sashes and window blinds wholesale. Two years later, just after the third child came into the family, William changed employment one more time. He and a partner, S.E. Cormany, bought a piece of property in Reed City, Osceola County, Michigan. The property encompassed one and a quarter acre. They built a new sawmill that was sixty-five feet by two hundred feet in size. They also constructed a brick edifice that housed the engine for the milling operation. When they had their mill up and running, they could handle sixty thousand feet of lumber per day. Additionally, they produced wooden boxes for shipments of goods, filling two train car loads every week. William and his partner took on fifteen employees.

Within six months, the mill was running efficiently, and William bought out his partner's share in the business. He took on another partner, W.W. Faster, who remained with him until July 1884. William then became the sole owner of the mill. He was the father of four children now. In addition to planing lumber and producing shipping boxes, William was a general lumber contractor and wholesale dealer.

In later years, the mill specialized in milling lumber for flooring. William's son Samuel took over as the superintendent of the firm upon William's retirement, though William remained active in the firm until 1915, when he was sixty-four years old. He was still the owner of the mill as he approached his seventieth birthday. William Horner's death occurred on December 26, 1925. The family provider was able to pass the care of the family onto those for whom he had provided for nearly all of his life.

68

OSCODA COUNTY

An Ordinary Extraordinary Life

William M. Foley was born on June 20, 1862, in Roscommon County, Ireland. He immigrated with his parents and sister to the United States in 1865 on the first immigrant ship to arrive in New York after the Civil War. The family settled in Grand Haven, Ottawa County, Michigan. When William was ten years old, both of his parents died. William and his sister, Winnie, were sent to live with an uncle who was not kind to them. William ran away to the "hobo jungle," where men traveled by foot or train, from town to town. One day, William came to the small community of Eastmanville, ten miles from Grand Haven. He met a man named Dr. Niles who invited William to come home with him to get something to eat. Dr. Niles and his wife invited William to stay with them. He accepted the offer but first returned to his uncle's farm for his sister.

William had never been to school, so Dr. Niles taught William to read using the Bible. When he turned sixteen, William left Dr. and Mrs. Niles and Winnie. He found work in lumber camps and labored as a lumberjack for several years. Eventually, William wanted to see Winnie again and Dr. and Mrs. Niles. William returned to Eastmanville, but upon his arrival, he learned that the doctor had sold his land and moved the family north to Grayling, Michigan. William traveled to Grayling, where the first person he met was a relative of Dr. Niles. The man, Dr. Palmer, told William that Dr. and Mrs. Niles lived nearby. He also told William that Winnie had passed away the previous year from consumption.

William decided that he would stay in the area. There was plenty of work for a lumberman. William was also experienced in breaking up log jams. The logs in this area were sent east along the Au Sable River to the town of Au Sable Oscoda at Lake Huron. William made the acquaintance of Pheba Elizabeth Bradley, who worked for Dr. and Mrs. Palmer. Lizzie, as she was called, had come to this area in 1880. Lizzie was given the opportunity to go to school, where she became qualified as a teacher. She taught in the spring and autumn months.

William and Lizzie were married in September 1894. They then went to live on an abandoned farm twenty miles east of Grayling. William worked for Dr. Niles on his farm. He and Lizzie had but one cow, which they lost when it fell into the river and drowned. This was a tragedy; along with providing their milk and butter, the cow had not been fully paid for yet. Lizzie taught in a school two miles from their farm. She had to cross the river by boat and then walk the rest of the way.

In January 1896, their first daughter was born. The family took possession of another abandoned farm across the river from their first home. There was a log cabin on the property, but it was in rough shape. Another daughter was born here in 1898. The family moved one last time to Big Creek Township in Oscoda County, where their third daughter was born in 1901. There was

Pioneer log cabin. *Authors' collections.*

a partially built cabin on this property. William and his neighbors finished the construction, and the family moved in.

William decided to raise cattle and sheep on their farm, and Lizzie churned butter that William sold in Grayling. He transported the butter using a horse and wagon. The journey took two days, fourteen hours each way. William purchased the family's groceries from the butter profits, but daily life was a continual struggle for the family. One day, William sighted a floating cook shack coming along the river. The shack came to rest in one of the farm fields, so William hitched up his team and retrieved the shack, towing it to the creek that ran in front of their cabin. He tethered it securely and then cut a hole in each end, allowing the water to flow. Lizzie used the shack to keep her butter, milk and cream cool.

In November 1913, Lizzie gave birth to a son. The baby was named after William. William and Lizzie continued to live their ordinary extraordinary lives until the end of their days.

69

OTSEGO COUNTY

I Will Make a Place for Us

Allan Briley was born in England in 1835. He was five years old when he and his foster parents immigrated to the United States. After their arrival, they settled in Providence, Rhode Island. Allan's foster father first found work in a woolen mill, then, a few years later, the family moved to Toronto. Here, they ran a hotel. When Allan was twenty-two years old, in 1857, he and Sarah Cummings married. Sarah was twenty years old. She was born in Canada to Thomas and Ellen McKnight Cummings, who had emigrated from County Down, Ireland. Allan and Sarah lived on a farm in Perth County, Canada. Allan wanted to buy another farm once their family was growing, but he needed money for the land. When Sarah was expecting their sixth child, Allan told her that he and two other men were going to California to find work lumbering and mining. Upon his return, he would have the money needed to buy another farm.

The three men set out in 1865, on a journey lasting many weeks. They had to sail around Cape Horn and then north to California. The men were away for four years; during this time, Sarah cared for her six children. Allan did purchase a larger farm when he returned where the family lived for five years. In 1875, Allan sold the farm in order to open a shop selling general merchandise. He overextended his credit which caused the business to fail. There were three more children in the family by this time, so Allan left his family again to find another home for them.

In 1878, Allan crossed Lake Huron into Michigan and made his way to Lapeer County. Allan arrived in Michigan in the springtime, when mosquito eggs were hatching. Many people who were bitten by the insects came down with ague (malaria), suffering recurring fevers and chills. Some people died from their affliction. Those who survived knew that the ague could strike again. Allan did not want to settle in this area. He boarded a Michigan Central Railroad train and rode it to the end of the line, which was Gaylord, Michigan, in Otsego County.

Allan acquired a homestead. The Homestead Act of 1862 offered land to new settlers; men who made a claim for land and lived on that land for five years while improving it—which generally meant cutting the trees and turning the soil to farming—then became the legal owners. After the Civil War, the U.S. government wanted to encourage settlement in Michigan. Veterans were allowed to homestead on 160 acres of land. Nonveterans could have 80 acres.

Otsego County was forested in white pine trees. After Allan claimed his homestead, he cut a trail through ten miles of forest. He followed a surveying line that had been marked years earlier. The trail had to be wide enough for a team of horses so that he could get a few rudimentary supplies in and the lumber he would need to build a shelter. Allan built a rough shanty, as he was on his own in the forest. His nearest neighbor lived ten miles away. That first winter, he saw only one other person, a timber cruiser, exploring the lumbering possibilities in the region.

Allan cleared ten acres of the homestead; then he built a house and barn. He hired himself out seasonally to earn money for supplies. Three years later, Sarah and eight of their children arrived in 1882. Eventually, they farmed 121 acres of land.

As the years passed, more settlers began homesteading around the Briley farm. There was talk of organizing into a separate township, with Allan supporting the idea. When a new township was officially organized, it was called Briley Township after Allan Briley. Allan offered that first rough shanty he had lived in for a schoolhouse. The unofficial post office was in the Briley home. Out of the forest, after many years, Allan Briley had made a home for his family. The intrepid immigrant pioneer died on November 19, 1915. Sarah Briley, stalwart immigrant partner, passed away on December 5, 1910.

70

OTTAWA COUNTY

Answering the Call

Charles Scott was born on December 18, 1822, at Little Britain in New Windsor Township, Orange County, New York. His parents were Alexander and Miriam Buchanan Scott. Alexander Scott's grandfather, Francis Scott of County Longford, Ireland, sailed in 1729 to New York on a ship chartered by Colonel Charles Clinton, also of County Longford. The ship was the *George and Ann*. Its owner was Gerald Cruise, another Irishman. Colonel Clinton had paid the fares for a number of his relatives, friends and other people. The *George and Ann* was one of seven ships that set sail from Belfast in May 1729. The reason for the exodus was the discrimination that Presbyterians experienced under the English government. Ministers encouraged followers to immigrate en masse to America, where they hoped to set up new congregations. In 1729, in Philadelphia, three to four ships carrying hundreds of Irish Presbyterian passengers arrived daily.

On May 9, 1729, Colonel Clinton and his party boarded the ship. There were about 180 passengers on board. The *George and Ann* was not fortunate in its crossing. The voyage was rough. Sickness and disease were rampant. Of the original number, more than 80 perished during the crossing. Two of Colonel Clinton's own children were among the first to die from an outbreak of measles. The voyage lasted twenty-three weeks. Originally, the ship was bound for New Castle, Delaware. Instead, it arrived at Cape Cod, Massachusetts, on October 4, 1729.

Francis Scott and the other survivors traveled to Ulster County, New York, in the spring of 1731. They made their settlement in Little Britain, about eight miles from the Hudson River and sixty miles from the city of New York. Francis took up farming. He and Eleanor McDowell married and raised their family in Blaggs Clove, Ulster County. His grandson Alexander grew up here and also became a farmer. Alexander's wife, Miriam, grew up on a nearby farm.

Alexander's son Charles received a common school education, which led him to set his mind on attending college. He entered Rutgers University in 1840. Four years later, Charles graduated from Rutgers with the highest honors. Charles planned to travel to Mexico and South America, but he first took a job as a private tutor in Adam's Run, near Charleston, South Carolina. While he was there, Charles experienced a religious conversion. He enrolled in the Theological Seminary of the Reformed Dutch Church in New Brunswick, New Jersey.

In 1851, Charles was licensed as a minister of the Reformed Dutch Church. One year earlier, he and Maria R. Stella had married. Charles accepted a position in the town of Shawangunk near his home in Ulster County. Charles and Maria moved to Shawangunk and began to raise a family. Eventually, they raised six children. Charles ministered at Shawangunk for fifteen years.

In 1866, the Reformed Dutch Church received a state charter for a liberal arts college to be established in Ottawa County, Michigan. The institution was named Hope College, located in Holland, Michigan. Charles was appointed professor of chemistry and natural history, so the family moved to Holland. Three years later, the college inaugurated a theology department with Charles as its lecturer. He taught church history, church government and archaeology, as well as general history.

In 1878, Charles was appointed vice president of the college. He was also in charge of administration and was the chair of the Department of Mental and Moral Philosophy. The financial situation of the college was precarious. Debts had mounted as expenses had outweighed the revenue brought in by student enrollment. Charles worked diligently to overcome the outstanding debts and to increase enrollment. In 1880, Charles was named the president of Hope College, a position he held for the remainder of his life. He continued lecturing while serving as president. Charles also served as the president of the General Synod of the Reformed Dutch Church. He received an honorary doctor of divinity degree from the University of New York. Charles answered a call to serve, which he did until his death on November 1, 1893.

71

PRESQUE ISLE COUNTY

Iron, Wood, Coal

Lemuel Crawford was born on December 15, 1805, in the village of Florida, Schoharie County, New York. His parents, Andrew and Elizabeth Dunham Crawford, were New England settlers originally from Ireland. When Lemuel was fourteen, he was left on his own. His father died, and his mother remarried. He found work in an iron foundry as a molder, learning the many steps to making molds for iron castings. The work required great strength and concentration. Lemuel worked in the foundry for six years.

In 1826, Lemuel accepted a position with the Geauga Furnace Company in Painesville, Ohio. He was the superintendent of the patterns and molding department. Lemuel stayed with the company for six years, during which time he and Louisa Murray married on July 29, 1832. The following year, Lemuel and Louisa moved to Detroit, where they lived for six years. Three of their four children were born there.

In 1837, the Board of Navy Commissioners convened to organize a system of lighthouses along the Great Lakes. The commission appointed P.J. Pendergast to select the sites along the lakes where lighthouses would be built. Traveling along the Lake Huron shoreline, Pendergast came to Presque Isle Harbor. In his report, Pendergast wrote, "This is an excellent harbor, and ought to be provided with a light to show vessels how to enter it in a stormy night. All the steamboats up and down the lake stop here for wood. The light if erected ought to be a colored one."

The next year, Congress appropriated $5,000 to build the first Michigan lighthouse on Presque Isle. Lemuel heard about Presque Isle and decided to move his family there in 1839. The Crawford family were the first nonindigenous settlers on Presque Isle. Lemuel built a dock and a store and a house for his family. The land was covered in dense forest that included massive white pine trees and smaller hardwood trees. Lemuel sold cordwood from the hardwood trees, which was used as fuel in the steamship boilers. All of the steamships stopped at his dock to take on fuel.

The next year, when the lighthouse was finished, an operator was needed, so Lemuel operated the lighthouse for five weeks until the permanent keeper, Henry Woolsey, arrived. In that same year, a government surveying party landed at Presque Isle. Among the surveyors was David D. Oliver. He and the others were surveying land that would become Alpena County. They had traveled to Presque Isle by canoe in hopes of meeting a steamship heading south on Lake Huron. When the survey party arrived at Lemuel's dock, he came to meet them. Dr. Oliver later recorded that first meeting: "The improvements at Presque Isle were owned by Lemuel Crawford… and consisted of a dock, store, and frame dwelling, a log barn, and a few log shanties. They were all built on Uncle Sam's land, which had not yet been surveyed."

Land that had not been surveyed was owned by the state, so Lemuel did not own the land or the trees that he cut and sold. It was not until 1844 that Lemuel actually purchased any land, becoming the first inhabitant of Presque Isle to own land in the county.

In 1846, Lemuel sold his business in Presque Isle so that he could pursue business in the coal trade. The family moved to Cleveland, Ohio. Lemuel invested $40,000 in the Chippewa Coal Mines of the Mahoning Valley. The supply of coal appeared limitless and was suited for blast furnaces. He continued to buy more land adjacent to the Chippewa Mines. Lemuel also began mining coal that was suited for steamship fuel. He had mining operations along the Ohio River, near Steubenville and in Orange County, Pennsylvania.

The coal mines made Lemuel a very wealthy man. In 1851, he branched out into the manufacturing of pig iron, which was essential for the production of steel. Eventually, Lemuel decided to invest in ships fueled by his coal. The ships transported grain along the Great Lakes. Lemuel Crawford lived the remainder of his life in Cleveland and died on June 30, 1868. He partook of the natural resources of the land, and they became his prosperity.

72

ROSCOMMON COUNTY

Like Father, Like Son

William R. Johnston, and his son, William F. Johnston, were both born in Peterborough, Ontario, Canada. In many ways, their lives followed parallel paths. Both men were sons of Irish immigrants—the father, whose parents had emigrated from Ireland, and the son, whose mother was also an Irish immigrant. William R. Johnston was born on December 12, 1840. His parents, William and Catherine Reynolds Johnston, were farmers. When they arrived in Canada, they took up farming again in Peterborough. William and Catherine raised ten children. When their son William reached twenty-one years of age, he left home. He found work in a lumber camp. After working as a lumberman for some years, he found work on the railroad.

Through hard work and frugal living, William was able to accumulate some savings. He and Mary Jane Brown married in 1864, when William was twenty-four years old. Their only child, William F. Johnston, was born on March 1, 1870. The family lived in Peterborough for seven years. In 1877, William decided to move his family to northern Michigan, where there was plenty of work for lumbermen and railroad men.

William became a foreman on the Michigan Central Railroad. He worked in northern Michigan towns for three years. In 1880, the family came to Roscommon County, settling in the village of Roscommon. The population of the village was 511. One year later, William was elected village marshal. After his term was over, William purchased 360 acres of land two miles away from the village. The land was unimproved, covered in stumps and scrub. Over the next fifteen years, the land was cleared and cultivated. William also took on business in logging and timber sales. He was appointed the supervisor of Gerrish Township. He also served as a justice of the peace and the county superintendent of the poor farm.

William F. Johnston was ten years old when the family settled in Roscommon. He received a basic education in the village school. When young William had gone as far as he could in the local school, he enrolled in the Michigan Agricultural College, located in East Lansing, Michigan. The college was established in 1855, the first agricultural college in the United States. William entered college in 1888. The following year, he was appointed to the post of clerk for the Committee on Railroads in the Michigan legislature. That position lasted through the legislative session of the year. In 1890, William returned home to assist his father on the farm. The next spring, he accepted a job as the bookkeeper for Charles Blanchard, a lumberman in Roscommon County. He worked for Blanchard until his lumber mill closed in the autumn.

On July 7, 1894, William and Alberta Mallory married. Alberta was a Michigan native from St. Clair County. That same year, William was elected the county clerk and also the Roscommon County register of deeds. He also held the title of school inspector. For a time, he also served as a justice of the peace, as his father did. William and Alberta had three children, a firstborn son named William, followed by a daughter and another son. Only their son Stanley grew to adulthood. Like his father, he attended the Michigan Agricultural College, where he was the president of the Union Board of Governors in 1918. After his marriage to Laura Collingwood in 1921, their firstborn son was named William.

As the twentieth century dawned, the elder William continued to farm until he met a tragic end. He was struck by a Michigan Central Railroad train on May 5, 1912. Young William had been appointed postmaster in the county two years earlier. He gave up his position when he and Alberta moved to the town of Paw Paw, in Van Buren County, to be closer to their son Stanley and his family. William served as an agricultural agent in Van Buren County.

The William Johnstons learned from their fathers and taught their sons to be hardworking and industrious wherever their lives led them.

73

SAGINAW COUNTY

Back to the Farm

Michael and Catherine Commins McCartney emigrated from County Louth, Ireland in 1848. When they arrived in New York Harbor, they boarded a boat heading up the Hudson River to Albany. In Albany, Michael and Catherine traveled the Erie Canal to Buffalo. In Buffalo, they boarded a boat that carried them across Lake Erie to Milan, Ohio. Michael had an aunt living in Milan who offered them a place to stay while they got settled. Milan was the second-largest wheat shipping port in the world thanks to the canal that connected the town to Lake Erie. Michael found work in one of the many factories in Milan. He and Catherine and their growing family lived in the town. In 1865, their tenth child was born. She was called Catherine Victoria, known as Kitt.

The next year, when railroad tracks were laid, Milan was bypassed. The canal was put out of business, along with many factories. The McCartney family moved from the village and became tenant farmers on land two miles west of Milan. Three more children were born.

When Kitt was sixteen years old, her father was able to buy land. He purchased eighty acres two miles west of the village of Oakley in Saginaw County, Michigan, for $1,600. Kitt, her six sisters and their mother rode the train to Oakley. Her father and brothers made the journey in a horse-drawn wagon.

Kitt became a farmer and a schoolteacher after the family's arrival. She taught in Brady Township, where the farm was located, and in nearby Chapin Township. Kitt alternated teaching with her brother Denis. Kitt taught the

Kitt McCartney (*lower left*) and her sisters. *Authors' collections.*

fall sessions during harvest time; Denis taught the winter session. Their pay supplemented the crops (oats, wheat, barley, potatoes) and livestock (pigs, chickens, cows) that the family farm produced.

As the children grew up, some left the farm. Kitt and her sister Julia each married one of the Carmody brothers, but Kitt's husband, James, died a few months after their wedding. Kitt had to go back to the farm. Her life

Kitt McCartney with niece Geraldine McCartney. *Authors' collections.*

became the farm and her family. When her brother Denis's wife died of consumption, Kitt helped raise their baby daughter, Mary, on the farm. When her younger sister Anna suffered a stroke, Kitt took care of her on the farm. When her older sister Alice could no longer work as a servant in Chicago, she, too, came back to the farm to be cared for by Kitt. When Denis's second wife had seven children at home with her, Kitt traveled to Owosso, ten miles away, to help care for the children. Kitt also took care of her older brother Patrick, who was not able to live independently.

Kitt kept the farm going as the wider world was changing around her. She went to Owosso to buy an automobile, and the car dealer taught her to drive. Kitt drove back to the farm, and when she arrived, she realized that she did not know how to turn the car off. Kitt drove the car around her fields until it ran out of gas.

In 1928, Kitt mortgaged the farm for $400 to the Chesaning State Bank. She was the last McCartney family member living on the farm, trying to manage it on her own. The note was due in three years. In 1931, during the Great Depression, Kitt could not meet the mortgage payment. The farm was auctioned off from the east steps of the Saginaw County Courthouse. Kitt could no longer "go back to the farm." Her niece Mary took her into her home in Oakley.

When Kitt was in her nineties, she went to live with the Little Sisters of the Poor at their convent/rest home in Grand Rapids, Michigan. Some days, her relatives in the Oakley area received a telephone call telling them that Kitt had been seen walking north along the highway from Owosso to Oakley. She had slipped away and taken the bus to Owosso, undaunted by the ten-mile walk back to the farm.

Kitt passed away in 1958, the last of the thirteen children of Irish immigrant parents who had come to America over one hundred years earlier.

74

ST. CLAIR COUNTY

The Squire

James Cogley was born on August 5, 1840, in Kilmore Quay, County Wexford, Ireland. He was the sixth child of nine born to Patrick and Mary Murphy Cogley. Kilmore Quay was only forty miles away from Vinegar Hill, once the headquarters of the United Irishmen and the site of a battle against British forces in 1798. During the famine year of 1847, Patrick and Mary decided to immigrate to Canada with their children. The journey was perilous, and the ship was overcrowded. Patrick and Mary's four-year-old twins died during the crossing. After the ship landed at Quebec, the family made their way to the town of Belleville, which was a center for lumbering. Patrick bought land for a farm. He and the older children built a log cabin and cleared the land for farming. They lived here for eight years.

In 1855, Patrick sold the farm and moved his family to Michigan. Two more daughters had joined the family. After crossing Lake Huron, they came to the town of Port Huron. Patrick purchased 320 acres of dense forest land in Kenockee Township, which he and his sons began clearing. In the first year, they cleared 60 acres. Eventually, another 160 acres were cleared.

When James turned fifteen years old, he wanted to become a blacksmith. He was apprenticed to S.S. Eaton in Memphis, Michigan, thirteen miles from home. James was a fast learner, and after three years, he became a journeyman blacksmith, traveling to Detroit to find work. After five years, James returned to Memphis. He hoped to start his own business.

James entered into a partnership with a man by the name of Frank E. Spencer. James carried out the blacksmithing work for their firm, which also manufactured wagons and buggies. The two men were very successful. The following year, 1864, James and Ellen Furlong of Detroit married. They made their home in Memphis. After four years, James bought out his partner's share of the business. He continued on his own for another two years. Then he sold out in order to buy a farm in Kenockee Township.

James began farming eighty acres but also kept blacksmithing. Two years later, he bought seven lots of property at Emmett Station, coinciding with the arrival of the railroad and regular train service. The family moved to the village of Emmett. James built two business properties and two residences. He also invested in a foundry, blacksmith and carriage shop. The firm was called the Emmet Farm Implement and Buggy Manufacturing Establishment. He continued to build houses and buildings for businesses in the village. He and Ellen were the parents of six children.

In 1872, James was appointed a justice of the peace, a position he retained for eighteen years. He also became a director on the local school board. He presided at the meetings of the village board and served as the Emmett Township treasurer for four years. In 1890, his son James entered into business with him. Two years later, they opened a hardware and implement store in conjunction with the foundry-smith-carriage business. Business was so good that a second store was opened in Memphis. Young James managed the Memphis business. Son George took up blacksmithing like his father. The enterprises came to be called Cogley and Sons, known throughout the county.

On August 29, 1910, while walking across his yard, James slipped and fell. He did not seem badly hurt, though he took to his bed. Later that evening, he suffered severe abdominal pains. Three physicians came to attend to him, but they could not relieve his distress. He was aware that he was fading and imparted final words to those around him: "I did not expect to be called now. But if it is God's will, I am ready." He had only recently celebrated his seventieth birthday. He was known by those who loved and respected him as the "Squire." The local newspaper obituary referred to him as "one of St. Clair County's pioneers and the best known and well-beloved citizen of Emmett."

75

ST. JOSEPH COUNTY

In Her Spare Time

Martha Dunnette was born in London, Ontario, on March 18, 1847. Her parents were the Reverend Samuel, and Catherine Philip Dunnette. Her father, an author of several books on theology, emigrated from England. When Martha was only a few years old, the family moved to Oakland Township in St. Joseph County, Michigan. Her father became the pastor of the local Baptist congregation, and Martha and her siblings attended a log school located next to the Baptist church. Martha began teaching school when she was sixteen years old. She continued her own education by reading widely from a range of noted literary writers. She read the works of William Shakespeare and the poems of Will Carlton. She studied the writings of George Bancroft and David Hume.

In 1873, Martha and John Culbertson married. John was the son of James Culbertson, an immigrant from County Donegal, Ireland, who had settled in Nottawa Township in St. Joseph County in 1834. James improved 215 acres of farmland, that, on his death in 1869, went to John. John engaged in general farming but also had an interest in the production and manufacturing of essential oils. He traveled widely throughout the United States, Central America and Europe. The large house that James built became the home of John, Martha and their children.

During this time, John had cause to bring litigation against a business associate. Martha began studying the law in the areas of tariffs, transportation of goods and financial matters in general. She became a knowledgeable advocate for John's case. The litigation continued for seven years and then was taken to the Supreme Court, where the judges decided in favor of the Culbertsons. They recovered thousands of dollars. From this venture, it became well known among their friends and associates that Martha was a force of intellectual expertise. She became an expert in matters of political economy. She was not timid to voice her thoughts and opinions. Even those who did not agree with her respected her well-thought-out opinions. One Republican representative to Congress from St. Joseph County said of Martha: "Though not personally acquainted with Mrs. Culbertson, yet I know her by reputation, and she is a lady of high character and ability, and worthy of confidence."

Martha championed the newly formed Union Party. She gave a speech in Cincinnati on behalf of the party that was well received, both for its demonstration of her knowledge about tariffs and finance and for her use of humor and wit, which carried the audience along with her. A reporter for the *Chicago Times* present at the meeting later remarked, "That woman is a serpent of tariff and finance." Martha was pressed by delegates in Michigan and other states to speak at their meetings, sharing her knowledge and her presence, but she demurred. She wished instead to return to her home and family, where she could help her husband with his business interests.

John Culbertson did not join in with Martha as she campaigned for various candidates or went to political meetings. He supported her but remained, at heart, a farmer all of his days. Their farm prospered through the years. As the nineteenth century drew to its close, Martha and John suffered a tragedy in the loss of their son, Corporal Sherman Culbertson, a soldier serving in the United States war against Spain. Though Secretary of State John Hay had said of the conflict, "This was a splendid little war," for the Culbertsons, their family paid a high price.

Martha Dunette Culbertson married the son of an Irish immigrant. She graciously performed all that was expected of a woman, wife and mother during the nineteenth century. In her spare time, she distinguished herself as an educator, an authority on matters of business and finance, a politician and a pursuer of justice for all. She passed away on September 5, 1922, having set the bar high for all those who followed in her footsteps.

76

SANILAC COUNTY

Fire!

A ndrew W. O'Keefe was born in Lanark County, Ontario Province, Canada, on August 7, 1845. His parents were John and Bridget Walsh O'Keefe. His father emigrated from County Cork, Ireland, and his mother was born in Ontario. Andrew grew up on a farm. He was the firstborn child of nine in the O'Keefe family.

In 1867, Andrew came to Sanilac County, Michigan. He began teaching school in the town of Lexington. After one term, he moved to Huron County, where he taught school for another term. He was also the bookkeeper for the owner of a sawmill. In 1869, Andrew moved to the village of Forestville, back in Sanilac County. He worked as a bookkeeper and salesman for Isaac Green, who owned a mercantile store.

Extensive lumbering in this region resulted in fields full of stumps and piles of scrub and brush. Farmers clearing their land built small fires to clean up the detritus. As the hot, dry summer of 1871 continued, these small fires began to combine. The hot air they generated rose, causing the wind to blow. The wind blew inland rather than out over Lake Huron, carrying embers and hot ashes. There was plenty of fuel in their path, as the inland region was less settled than the lakeshore. Farmers tried to put out any sparks wherever they saw them. On the afternoon of October 8, 1871, the wind strengthened.

Suddenly, many smaller fires all came together in a roaring inferno. At first, farmers tried to save their barns and animals. Then, they tried to save their homes. Quickly, all thoughts were only of saving lives. Mothers grabbed their children, shouting for older children to carry or pull younger ones along. One father found his little son hiding under his crib, too terrified to call out. He grabbed his son and then raced outside. The only possible safe place was the well in the yard, twelve feet down with three feet of water at the bottom. The family climbed in, and three more families crowded inside too. There they stayed through the night and the next day.

In Forestville, people were fighting the fire on one side of the village when it came at them from the other side. Anyone who could get to the lake went into the water. People drove their wagons into the water. High waves hurled people back onto the beach. Every building except for one saloon was destroyed. Entire families were killed. People were blinded for life. Many lost limbs, hands and feet to the flames.

Andrew O'Keefe lost everything except for the clothes on his back. He had purchased several lots in Forestville and built a hotel. Relief committees were organized, but it was difficult to get food, clothing and tools to victims since the roads were blocked by fallen trees. People who needed medical care had to wait many days. The only food readily available was meat due to the thousands of cattle and other animals that were victims of the fire. Many people lost their lives. Thousands were left homeless.

Andrew rebuilt the Forestville hotel in 1872. He and Agnes Towel, a daughter of Irish immigrants, married on June 10, 1872, in Minden City. She had been a teacher before her marriage. In 1873, Andrew was appointed postmaster of Forestville. He managed his hotel until the year 1880, when he won the election for the county clerk. He served three terms as county clerk.

And then, ten years later, the Great Fire of 1881 struck. Once again, smaller fires had been accumulating, but people thought it was too early for strong winds to form. On September 5, 1881, what seemed like a cyclone developed. Within four hours, the fire had traveled over the entirety of Sanilac County. The fire ceased only when there was literally nothing left to burn. Three hundred people lost their lives. Fourteen thousand people lost everything they had.

By 1900, the O'Keefes were living in the city of Port Huron. Andrew worked as a clerk and bookkeeper. Agnes passed away in 1901, and Andrew died on July 23, 1908. What fire destroyed, he rebuilt, one of the truly fortunate residents of Sanilac County.

77

SCHOOLCRAFT COUNTY

Finding a Place in History

John McCanna was born on April 27, 1847, in Swanton, Franklin County, Vermont. His parents were Henry and Nancy Ann O'Kane McCanna. Henry, born in Tullagh, County Donegal, Ireland, immigrated to Canada and then crossed over into Sandy Hill, New York. He and Nancy Ann married there in 1845. They moved to Swanton, where logging was the biggest industry. Nancy Ann gave birth to John, followed two years later by another son, Henry. In 1850, the family left Swanton. They came to Painted Post in Steuben County. Over the next eighteen years, six more children were born into their family.

Henry found work as a sawyer in nearby Gangs Mill. The name of their village, Painted Post, came from a post with carvings on it that had been placed at the junction of three rivers. The carvings seemed to have been made by members of the Seneca tribe who were in the region. Early explorers painted the post and used it as a meeting place.

In 1861, when the Civil War began, Henry volunteered with the 23rd New York Infantry. John, at fourteen years old, wanted to volunteer also. He went to Washington, D.C., with the 107th New York Regiment, hoping to become a drummer. When Henry found out, he traveled to Washington, D.C., found the camp of the 107th and ordered John to return home to help his mother with the five younger children. John returned home and stayed there for the next three years.

When John was seventeen, he once again went to join the 107th New York Infantry. His father had joined that same regiment earlier in the year. Henry and John shared the same tent. Both served under General Sherman when he led the march from Atlanta to Savannah, Georgia, a distance of 285 miles. They survived the war and returned home to Painted Post.

Henry returned to lumbering, but John left Painted Post in 1867, moving to Harrisville, in Alcona County, Michigan, where he found work as a sawyer. Two years later, John and Anna Hogue married. In 1870, John's parents and his brothers, Henry, Charles and Alexander, also moved to Harrisville. They all worked in a sawmill. John's parents moved farther north to the village of Manistique in Schoolcraft County in 1878. John moved his family there the following year. Everyone was following the lumber industry as it moved farther north, where the forests had not yet been harvested. Both Henry and John were employed by the Chicago Lumber Company. Henry was a sawyer, and John was the operator of a lathe mill.

In 1882, John was elected sheriff of Schoolcraft County. As sheriff, John maintained the jail, which contained five cells used to hold prisoners. A wood-fired furnace heated the building. In 1884, fire destroyed the jail. Sheriff McCanna had to transport prisoners to the jail at St. Ignace, nearly one hundred miles away. The next year, a new jail was built.

Next to the jail was the house provided for the sheriff and his family. John's tenure lasted until the end of 1885. In 1886, John's brother Henry took over as sheriff. Henry filled a two-year term with his brother William serving as undersheriff. John and his family remained in Manistique until he took charge of a lumber mill in Green Bay, Wisconsin. When the lumber ran out, the family of ten moved once more, in 1904, to Ontonagon County, Michigan. John worked as a filer in a sawmill. He sharpened the saws for the lumbermen, often working all night long so the saws were ready in the morning.

John worked in the lumber industry until his retirement. He passed away on August 7, 1930, followed by Anna four years later. John's years as sheriff in Schoolcraft County earned him a place in the history of the county. As a soldier in the Civil War, he claimed a place in the history of the country. In the sawmills, he earned a place in Michigan's logging history.

78

SHIAWASSEE COUNTY

The Pioneer Kings

John and Bridget Murtaugh King married in the parish of Cloonglish in County Longford, Ireland. They had six children by the time the potato blight and land evictions made it difficult for people to survive. Bridget decided to ensure her family's survival, so she sailed to New York. She found work as a servant and was heard to say, "I do two women's work and want two women's pay." Bridget worked in New York City until 1849, when she had saved enough money to send for her husband and children.

The reunited King family traveled from New York to Michigan. One son, James, who was eighteen years old, remained in Detroit, where he found work as a molder, earning $1.75 per day. The rest of the family traveled to Flint Township in Genesee County, where they bought an unimproved farm. They began clearing the land. After four years, 25 acres were cleared. In 1853, they traded 40 acres plus $200 for 480 acres of land in Hazelton Township in Shiawassee County.

It took many years to improve their land. At times, John found his debts mounting. Once, his son Joseph, who had remained in Flint, paid his father's debts and was given 100 acres of the farm. Later on, John split the farmland in three ways for his sons, James and John, and a neighbor, Michael Conly. Young John added another 240 acres to his parcel. In 1860, he deeded his interest to Michael Conly. In 1862, Michael deeded his share to James.

During the Civil War, Joseph, James and young John joined the Union army. Joseph was captured and sent to Andersonville Prison. James wrote a letter to the War Department seeking information about him:

Commissary of prisoners Washington, D.C.

Dear Sir, I wish you would inform me about Joseph King, Co. K, 23rd Regiment, Michigan Infantry he was taken prisoner on the 27th of January A.D. 1864—and we heard he was taken to Andersonville Georgia and I would be very happy to hear from you if he is still alive or dead as I can get no accounts of him.

Yours,
James King

Joseph and eleven other soldiers eventually escaped. They made their way back to a Union regiment. Joseph, very ill, was sent to Detroit. He did not survive the waiting period before he was mustered out. James and young John survived and returned home.

Andersonville Prison Camp. *Public domain.*

James and Mary Jane Malloy married in 1860, and had ten children. When Mary passed away at age forty-nine in 1892, the oldest daughter, Maria, took over running the household. The household was known as a happy place. Many parties were held in the large house James built. The front parlor had seven doors leading from it, four of them to the outside. His farm was prosperous, and he was regarded as a leader in the community. People took to calling him, respectfully, "Old Jim." Many people mourned Old Jim's passing when he died on November 30, 1915.

Young John King was nearly eighteen when the family moved to Hazelton Township. He stayed at home, working with his father to improve the land until he reached the age of twenty-two. He then began hiring himself out as a laborer on other farms. In 1860, he built a frame house on his land. In 1861, he and Bridget Trainor married. Bridget was seventeen years old. She and John had two children, but neither survived. Bridget died when she was twenty-two.

In 1867, John married again. His second wife was Bridget Delehanty from County Clare, Ireland. She and John had fourteen children. Their farm was the highest-assessed property in the township. They had a big house built for their large family, and all of their children were well educated. John served on the local school board. He was also the highway commissioner and the township treasurer. John suffered from asthma, which resulted in poor health for most of his adult years. He died before his fifty-seventh birthday on February 25, 1893.

The pioneer Kings helped to build a thriving farming community in Shiawassee County. They carried on, just as their ancestors had done before them.

79

TUSCOLA COUNTY

I Do the Job that Needs Doing

Thomas W. Keenoy traveled with his parents, Marcus and Susan McCabe Keenoy, and his siblings to the United States in the 1880s. He was born on May 21, 1869, in Castlerea, County Roscommon, Ireland. When the family arrived, they made their way to Michigan, where they took up farming in Greenleaf Township, Sanilac County. Thomas worked on the farm for a few years but then traveled to Detroit. He found work on the ships traveling the Great Lakes.

In 1893, over three thousand ships were carrying cargo and passengers on the Great Lakes. The cargo included iron and copper ores, lumber, wheat and other grains. There were continuous shipments of goods heading to East Coast cities and Chicago. Thomas found work on Lake Erie as a lookout and wheelman under Captain Archie McLachlin. Captain McLachlin came from a long line of sailors and captains of vessels on the Great Lakes. His father, Captain John McLachlin, ran tugboats in the Bay City area. His grandfather, another Archie McLachlin, had been on the Great Lakes ever since he arrived in the United States as a young man from Glasgow, Scotland. The younger Captain Archie McLachlin had command of the *City of Detroit* for several years. Thomas remained with Captain McLachlin for ten years. During this time, Thomas and Mary Ann Patrick decided to marry. Mary Ann was the daughter of Andrew and Mary Patrick, farmers in Ubly, Michigan, in Huron County. Thomas and Mary Ann made their home in Detroit. Mary Ann was sixteen years old when she married Thomas on February 3, 1893. She gave birth to four sons but died at twenty-four from tuberculosis.

After Mary's death, Thomas and his sons returned to Greenleaf Township. His father passed away two years later, on June 14, 1903. Thomas continued running the farm and married Harriet Lashinger. Harriet gave birth to a daughter and then, two years later, a son. Thomas's mother, Susan, went to live in Detroit with Thomas's brother Michael, a fireman. A few years later, the family moved from the farm to the village of Cass City in Tuscola County. Thomas was appointed the night watchman by the village president. The merchants wanted someone to patrol the village streets, keeping their stores safe at night. Thomas walked the village streets from dusk til dawn. He took his job seriously, wearing a policeman's hat and a silver star badge pinned to his shirt. He was armed and carried a billy club as well. Thomas checked each front and back door of the local businesses, making sure they were locked securely. He escorted inebriated and disorderly persons into the local jail, known as the hoosegow.

Tom, as the Cass City residents knew him, was a man with a compassionate heart. When he met a hungry person passing through the village, he would escort him to a local restaurant so that the man could get a hot meal. In the latter years of the 1920s, Tom was earning forty dollars per month. His position became more of a town marshal as the years passed. He patrolled the streets for over twenty years, retiring when he was eighty years old. Tom never lost his Irish brogue and brought it out in force every St. Patrick's Day. People liked to hear his songs and stories. Harriet Keenoy passed away in 1946 at the age of sixty-two. Tom moved to the Detroit area to live with his daughter Maria, as his health was not very good. He had done all the jobs that needed doing when he died on February 27, 1950.

80

VAN BUREN COUNTY

Keeper of the Light

James S. Donahue was born on March 18, 1842, in Addison County, Vermont. His parents, Manday and Nellie Loan Donahue, were Irish immigrants. When James was twelve years old, he joined a whaling ship as a cabin boy. James sailed for forty-four months, crossing the Pacific and Atlantic Oceans. When he returned, he worked in a machine shop in Lowell, Massachusetts. In 1861, James relocated to Detroit.

James enlisted as a private in Company A, Eighth Michigan Infantry. He was first engaged in battle at Hilton Head, South Carolina. He was hit by grapeshot in the shoulder at Charleston, South Carolina, in 1862. James was sent to the soldier's hospital on David's Island in New York. His recovery took six months. When he was discharged, James rejoined his regiment and was promoted to captain. On May 6, 1864, during the Battle of the Wilderness, James's left leg was pierced by a bullet and had to be amputated at the thigh. He was forced to resign from the army.

After the war, James moved to Seville Township in Gratiot County, where he took up farming. He and Sophia Oberlin married on June 17, 1872. In 1874, James applied for the position of lighthouse keeper in South Haven, Van Buren County. He received a return letter from the lighthouse board:

Mr. Donahue, we appreciated your service to our country, but we question your ability to carry out the duties of a lighthouse keeper. South Haven Lighthouse requires strength and coordination, which would be very difficult for a person crippled like yourself.

First South Haven Lighthouse, Van Buren County. *Historical Association of South Haven.*

James wrote a second letter:

> *Gentlemen, it is quite true that I was twice injured in the war, the second time losing a leg in the Battle of Wilderness, however, I am not crippled, as you assert. I am capable of carrying out any and all duties required of a lighthouse keeper and will gladly prove it to you if you will give me the opportunity to serve my country in this manner.*

The lighthouse board appointed James the second keeper at South Haven, and he began his appointment in September 1874. In March 1875, their son Edward was born.

The South Haven lighthouse was a wooden structure at the end of a three-hundred-foot-long pier at Lake Michigan. There was an elevated walkway since the pier was often coated in ice during the wintertime. James built a handrail along the walkway to help him reach the lighthouse. During inclement weather, James remained in the lighthouse, signaling ships with a hand-operated horn.

James kept a daily log of temperature, weather conditions, the names of incoming vessels and their owners, as well as a record of maintenance on the lighthouse. Entries included:

I went to the village councal one hour in the evening. My wife and brother was at the end of the pier blowing the fog horn and braut in the Steam Tug Miranda at eight-thirty P.M.

July 3, 1875: Rain and cloudy, wind moderate, lake smooth, the night dark, the weather warm—my wife died this afternoon at 4P.M., of lung disease.

July 4, 1875: Foggy, wind, the fog thick all day, the lake smooth, the night dark—I berryied my wife today at 4P.M.

James was widowed when Edward was four months old. The following year, James and Ann Kyme married. Six more children completed their family. James did not let his disability deter him. Often, he was the only person at the scene when disaster struck. James saved fifteen lives by jumping into the lake to bring people to safety. Once, James rescued two of his own sons. His bravery did not go unnoticed. He received a silver medal from the U.S. government in recognition of his service: "To Captain James S. Donahue: for bravely rescuing several persons in drowning, 1875–1879." The further inscription reads: "In testimony of heroic deeds in saving lives from the perils of the sea."

James Donahue with family and friends. *Historical Association of South Haven.*

One evening, James received several visitors. Fifty-two of the sailors and lake men of South Haven brought James a gift. He was presented with a gold medal inscribed, "Presented to Captain James S. Donahue by the seamen of South Haven March 18, 1885."

James maintained the lighthouse for thirty-five years, retiring in 1910. When he passed away on November 20, 1917, the keeper of the light was laid to rest with military honors.

81

WASHTENAW COUNTY

In a Surgeon's Care

Edward Batwell was born on June 1, 1828, in Charleville, County Cork, Ireland. He was the youngest of eight children born to Andrew and Helen Galway Batwell. The Batwell family had been in Charleville since the 1500s. Andrew Batwell was a seneschal, a royal officer overseeing judicial and administrative matters in the barony of Orery, where Charleville was located. He was also a captain in the English yeomanry, a branch of the military consisting of Irishmen serving the English government voluntarily.

Edward attended the Church of Ireland school in Charleville until the age of thirteen. In 1841, he was apprenticed to a local apothecary, Thomas Gorman, for five years. After this, Edward went to Dublin, where he enrolled in Trinity College in the Royal College of Surgeons. He graduated in 1849. He then went to London, where he studied at the Royal College of Physicians. After graduation, he was accepted as a member of the Royal College of Surgeons of London, England.

Home once again, Edward took the examination for admittance into England's navy. While awaiting his results, he decided to journey across the Atlantic to New York. He sailed from Queenstown in County Cork in November 1849 aboard the ship *Republic*. The crossing took five weeks. Instead of remaining in New York, Edward set out for Detroit soon after his arrival. He was so taken with Detroit he decided to remain. Six months later, Edward received word that he had been admitted into the English navy. He turned the appointment down and remained in Detroit. His money was nearly gone, so Edward opened a medical practice. He soon made a name for himself as a surgeon. He also made the acquaintance of a woman named Frances Delane, and on June 1, 1854, Edward and Frances married.

When the Civil War began, Edward was commissioned as a surgeon in the Irish Rifles. The regiment was later absorbed into the Fourteenth Michigan Infantry. He was named brigade surgeon in 1862 and responsible for administrative record keeping. He kept a record of the medical supplies and a weekly account of all the sick and wounded men. He kept track of the liquor allotted for purposes of anesthesia. He wrote a report after each battle, detailing the strength of the regiment and recording the numbers of wounded, killed or missing men. It fell to Edward to make battlefield decisions regarding injured soldiers.

Medical care for soldiers was mostly palliative in nature. Minor wounds were cleansed and bandaged. Surgeons had either opium or laudanum to give for pain. Anesthesia options were chloroform or ether. If neither was available, liquor was used. Wounded soldiers suffered from exposure as well as inadequate food and nutrition. Infected wounds were common. A leading cause of death was chronic diarrhea from parasites and other infectious agents, as well as unclean water.

In 1864, Edward was named the division surgeon in charge of the field hospital of the Second Division, Fourteenth Army Corps. Edward selected the location of the field hospital at a battle scene. He was the supervisor of the care and treatment injured men received. He maintained all of the medical records and made routine reports about hospital conditions. Edward was honored by the U.S. Senate for his "gallant and meritorious service" during the war. Shortly before he was mustered out, Edward was given the rank of lieutenant colonel.

After the war ended, Edward returned to Detroit. In 1866, he moved his family to the town of Ypsilanti, in Washtenaw County, where he opened a surgical practice. Edward was often called upon by his colleagues to consult or to attend a complicated surgical procedure.

In 1873, Edward helped to organize the Ypsilanti fire department. He also served as the Washtenaw County coroner and surgeon. He served as the town physician. Frances passed away in 1874, and eight years later, Edward married again. His second wife was Mary Carpenter. She and Edward had two daughters.

Edward Batwell was never healthy after the war. He was plagued with chronic digestive problems that prevented him from partaking of adequate nutrition. His body weakened with each passing year. The caring surgeon passed away on December 26, 1899.

82

WAYNE COUNTY

How Corktown Came to Be

Antoine de la Mothe Cadillac established Fort Pontchartrain in 1701 at a site on the Detroit River. The earliest settlement was a garrison that became a center for trading furs, which were transported on the river. Detroit, in Wayne County, remained a small settlement until European immigrants began arriving in the early 1800s. Many Irish immigrants found East Coast cities too crowded. Detroit, farther west, seemed full of opportunities. After the Erie Canal was completed in 1825, thousands of Irish immigrants traveled to Detroit.

The Irish immigrants settled on the east side of Detroit. They did not have their own church, but they were allowed to hold Mass in St. Anne's Church, established by early French settlers. In 1833, Father Bernard Cavanaugh persuaded a local man, Alpheus White, to repurpose a building that was for sale. Father Cavanaugh blessed the building and renamed it Most Holy Trinity Catholic Church. This church was home to the first Irish parish in the western United States. In 1834, when cholera was rampant in the town, the church became a hospital.

As more Irish immigrants came into Detroit, they eventually had to spread from the east side of the town. They began settling on the west side in an area referred to as the "Irish section." Most Holy Trinity Church was moved to the Irish section so parishioners could walk to services. Many of the immigrants were from County Cork, so the area came to be called Corktown.

George A. O'Keefe was born in County Cork, Ireland, around 1796. He was educated in England and at Trinity College in Dublin. George arrived in

New York in 1816 and made his way to Detroit, where he began practicing the law. He became a probate judge and was said to be "an Irish Gentleman in the truest and fullest sense, learned, cultured, brilliant and witty." George celebrated his Irish heritage. He was a founder of the St. Patrick's Society in 1829 and the president of the Friends of Ireland. He was the leader of the St. Patrick's Day festivities in Detroit for years. At the 1842 St. Patrick's Day banquet, held in the warehouse of the American Fur Company, George gave the welcoming remarks. Over eight hundred people were in attendance.

By the year 1853, one in seven residents of Detroit was an Irish immigrant. Corktown was home to 45 percent of Detroit's Irish population. However, even in Corktown, sometimes anti-Irish sentiments were heard and felt. One cause of anti-Irish feeling was the number of poor immigrants arriving daily. They were portrayed as job stealers, unlike professional men like George O'Keefe. At times, mobs ran through Corktown setting fires, vandalizing houses and beating the residents.

Most Holy Trinity Church's membership continued to grow, and a larger church was needed. Construction began in the mid-1850s and was completed by 1865. The new church served four thousand parishioners weekly. Not only were the Irish Catholics devout in their church attendance, but they were also adamant that their children would be well educated. In 1850, 74 percent of the children of Detroit's Irish immigrants between the ages of five and sixteen attended school.

In 1858, an Irishman was elected as Detroit's mayor. He was John Patton from County Down, Ireland, who immigrated with his family to New York in 1830. He arrived in Detroit in 1843. John opened a carriage factory on Woodward Avenue, a main thoroughfare of the city. He prospered and became a favorite among his fellow Irishmen for his ability to quote passages of literature and poetry, especially the poems of Robert Burns. John was also a member of St. Patrick's Benevolent Society, serving as its president. He was an organizer of the St. Patrick's Day parade, which had grown over the years to include thousands of people marching or lining the streets. The parade route wound through Corktown and along Woodward Avenue, ending at the cathedral of Saints Peter and Paul where everyone listened to a sermon on the life of Saint Patrick.

The Irish in Corktown became leading citizens and part of the industrious backbone of Detroit. They were proud of their Irish heritage and their place in the history of Wayne County.

83

WEXFORD COUNTY

An Orphan Makes His Way

William Kelley was born on January 25, 1845. When William was seven years old, he and his father immigrated to New York. The rest of the family perished during the famine years, but the two survived the ocean crossing. They found lodgings in the city upon their arrival. However, within a few weeks, William's father died, leaving William on his own.

By 1850, there were nearly 200,000 Irish immigrants in New York City. There were not many places for a child alone. Those who would survive the streets of New York had to find honest employment. A boy could find work in a factory feeding a coal fire for eight to twelve hours of the day. A boy could be hired to walk alongside a mule team on a canal route. The mules pulled barges loaded with goods for the city markets. Children were paid less than adults and so this saved bargemen money. Boys worked both day and night. The night shift was possible because there were pewter lanterns on board the barges. The boy and the mule team walked close to the canal banks. Frequently, lanterns exploded, causing terrible burns. There was no compensation for injuries, so a boy's best hope was to recover and get back to work.

Most people believed it was good for orphans to be employed because it kept them off the streets. Children without legal employment might become ragpickers, pickpockets or thieves or be taken in for prostitution. William somehow kept out of harm's way. In 1861, when he was sixteen, he enlisted in the Union army. He fought in the Battle of Bull Run at Manassas Junction in Virginia. He was taken prisoner and sent to Libby Prison in Richmond,

Hardwood logs at mill. *Michigan State University Archives and Historical Collections.*

Virginia. He was transferred to another prison in Salisbury, North Carolina. William was a prisoner for eleven months before being released during a prisoner exchange. Yet he made his way back to his regiment, with which he served until the end of the war.

After the war, William returned to New York City but soon headed west to Michigan. He took up farming near the town of Greenville in Montcalm County. In September 1870, he and Nancy Louisa Van Ness married. William and Nancy remained in Greenville for two years, but in August 1872, William sold his farm. He and Nancy relocated to Clam Lake in Wexford County. As a veteran, William was able to acquire 160 acres of land for homesteading. He and Nancy were among the first settlers to arrive in Clam Lake after passenger rail service began. They brought their young daughter with them.

Wexford County was soon experiencing the lumber boom that had been going on in the southern regions of Michigan. The county had not experienced the devastating fires that had occurred in Chicago, Wisconsin and the eastern region of Michigan in October 1871. Everywhere that the fires had consumed, lumber for rebuilding was needed. William began a profitable lumbering business in Clam Lake.

Eventually, he turned to real estate. He bought land and began to put up buildings for businesses. He was interested in seeing Clam Lake become a prosperous center of commerce. The town was renamed Cadillac in July 1877. William joined the local school board and became a member of the town council as well. He was a trustee of the local Presbyterian Church, to which he contributed much of his wealth.

On December 27, 1878, local residents were shocked to learn that William Kelley had died after a short illness. He was thirty-three years old. People in Cadillac continued to speak highly of him and wanted his name entered into the town's history as well as the history of Wexford County. An orphan had made his way home.

BIBLIOGRAPHY

Ancestry. ancestry.com.

Ask about Ireland. "The Battle of Carlow." www.askaboutireland.ie.

———. "The Story of the Wild Goose Lodge." www.askaboutireland.ie.

Austin, Dan. "Alexander Macomb Monument." Historic Detroit, www. historicdetroit.org.

Beaver Island Historical Society. "Beaver Island History." www.beaverisland.net.

Begin Tracing Your Irish Ancestry. "Presbyterian Exodus County Longford." www. from-Ireland.net.

Biographical History of Northern Michigan. Chicago: B.F. Bowen & Company, 1905.

Biographical Memoirs of St. Clair County, Michigan. Logansport, IN: B.F. Bowen Publishers, 1903.

Biographical Record of Houghton, Baraga, and Marquette Counties. Chicago: Biographical Publishing Company, 1903.

Biographical Sketches of Leading Citizens of Oakland County, Michigan. Chicago: Biographical Publishing Company, 1903.

Biographical Sketches: "History of Grand Rapids and Kent County, Michigan Containing Biographical Sketches of Prominent and Representative Citizens." N.p.: A.W. Bowen, 1900.

Briley, Gordon. "Allan Briley May Have Led Joburg Pioneers." *Herald Times Sesquicentennial*, August 20, 1937.

Britannica. "William Walker." www.britannica.com.

Brotherhood of Locomotive Engineers and Trainmen. "150th Anniversary Celebration." www.ble-t.org.

Bulkley, John. *History of Monroe County, Michigan.* Chicago: Lewis Publishing Company, 1913.

Buysse, Ellen. Interview by Patrick Commins and Elizabeth Rice, 2019.

Calhoun County, Michigan. "History of Calhoun County." www.calhouncountymi.gov.

Canadian Encyclopedia. www.thecanadianencyclopedia.ca.

Cass City Area Historical Society. "History of the Cass City Police Department." In *The Way It Was*, 33–34. Cass City, MI: Cass City Historical Society, 1996.

Cass City Chronicle. "Thomas Keenoy Obituary." February 28, 1950.

Charles O'Malley Biographical Papers. Clarke Historical Library, Central Michigan University. www.cmich.edu.

Chelsea Michigan Standard. "Hugh McCabe Obituary." December 2, 1909.

City of Manistique. "Sheriff John McCanna (1882–1885)." cityofmanistique.org.

Civil War Talk. "The History of Bugling." www.civilwartalk.com.

Coburn, Carol K., and Martha Smith. *Spirited Lives: How Nuns Shaped Catholic Culture and American History*. Chapel Hill: University of North Carolina Press, 2005.

Coldwater, Michigan. "History of Branch County." www.coldwater.org.

Coleman, Terry. *Passage to America*. London: Pimlico Publishing, 1972.

Cortez, Jan. "Mecosta Village." Morton Township, www.mortontownship.org.

Detroit Historical Society. "Timeline of Detroit." www.detroithistorical.org.

Diabolical, Judge S.B., and D.W. Kelley. *Past and Present of Clinton County, Michigan*. Chicago: S.J. Clarke Publishing Company, 1906.

Division of Military and Naval Affairs. "Annual Reports of the Bureau of Military Statistics." www.dmna.ny.gov.

Duck, Julieta. "Committee of Vigilance of San Francisco." Found SF, www.foundsf.org.

Eddy, Corbin. "Reverend Mother Agnes Gonzaga Ryan, C.S.J." In *Hidden Gems and Towering Tales, A Hancock, Michigan Anthology, 1863–2013*, by Laura Mahon and John S. Haeussler, 48-49. Hancock, MI: City of Hancock, 2013.

Ellis, Franklin. *History of Livingston County, Michigan*. Philadelphia: Everts & Abbott, 1880.

Encyclopedia.com. "Cattle Drives." www.encyclopedia.com.

———. "Government Land Policy." www.encyclopedia.com.

Fine, Sydney. *Frank Murphy: The Detroit Years*. Ann Arbor: The University of Michigan, 1975.

Foley, William, Jr. "Ausable River Genealogy." *Wilderness Chronicle*, n.d.

Freedman, Eric. *Pioneering Michigan*. Franklin, MI: Altwerger and Mandel Publishing Company, 1992.

Fuller, George Newman, ed. *Historic Michigan: Land of the Great Lakes*. Dayton, OH: National Historical Association, 1928.

Garrett, Bob. "Life in a Logging Camp." Michiganology. www.michiganology.org.

Gladwin County Record and Beaverton Clarion. "James Riley, Descendant of Gladwin County Pioneer Honored." June 22, 2016. www.gladwinmi.com.

Goodbody, Rob. "Quakers and the Famine." *History Ireland Magazine*, Spring 1998.

Harrison, John. "Charles O'Malley Renames Michigan Counties." Michigan State University, www.lib.msu.edu.

BIBLIOGRAPHY

Harrison, Timothy. "South Haven Lights." *Lighthouse Digest*, October 1999.

Hartwick, L.M., and W.H. Tuller. *Oceana County Pioneers & Business Men of To-Day*. Pentwater, MI: Pentwater News Steam Print, 1890.

Hiss Reet. "History of Thatching and Thatched Roofs." www.hiss-reet.de.

History Link 101. "Threshing Machines." www.historylink101.com.

History of American Women. "Jane Johnston Schoolcraft." www.womenhistoryblog.com.

"The History of Blacksmithing." *Forge Magazine*, March 2017. www.forgemag.com.

History of Kalamazoo County, Michigan with Illustrations and Biographical Sketches of Its Men and Pioneers. Philadelphia: J.B. Lippincott & Company, 1880.

History of Ottawa County. Chicago: H.R. Page & Company, 1882.

History of Poverty and Homelessness in New York City. www.nychomelesshistory.org.

History of St. Clair County, Michigan. Chicago: Andreas and Company, 1883.

History of Steuben County. Syracuse: D. Mason & Company, 1896.

History of the Great Lakes in Two Volumes. Chicago: J.G. Beers and Company, 1899.

History of Tuscola and Bay Counties, Michigan. Chicago: H.R. Page & Company, 1883.

History of Wexford County, Michigan. Chicago: B.F. Bowen, 1903.

Hope College. "History of Hope College." www.hope.edu.

Images of Michigan. "Images of the Pioneers of Osceola County: William Horner." www.imagesofmichigan.com.

Immaculate Conception Catholic Church. "A Brief History of Our Parish." www.iccatholic.org.

Infomercantile. "Ancient Order of United Workmen." www.infomercantile.com.

Ingalls, E.S. *Centennial History of Menominee County—1876*. Madison: University of Wisconsin, n.d.

———. The Iron Mines of Menominee County, Michigan. Iron Mountain, MI: Mid-Peninsula Library Federation, 1972.

Kellogg, Angela, and Cody Beemer. *Harrison*. Charleston, SC: Arcadia Publishing, 2014.

Koch, Sandra. "Forgotten Community: Irishtown." *In the Middle*, November/December 2004.

Lankton, Larry. *Cradle to Grave: Life, Work and Death at the Lake Superior Copper Mines*. New York: Oxford University Press, 1991.

LaPointe, Katherine. "The Story Behind the Stump." Mason County History Companion. www.ludingtonmichigan.net.

Lemmor, Victor F. "Richard Langford and the Discovery of the Colby Mines," contributed to "Ghost Mines of the Gogebic Range," *Youngstown Steel Bulletin*, October 1966. From the collected writings of Victor Lemmor, 1898–1974. quod. lilb.umich.edu.

Library of Congress. "Ancient Arabic Order of the Nobles of the Mystic Shrine." www.loc.gov.

Lighthouse Friends. "South Haven Pier Lighthouse." www.lighthousefriends.com.

Litwiller, Lisa Yanick. "Living in History." *Morning Sun*, www.themorningsun.com.

Loomis, Bill. "Irish Helped Form Detroit for Centuries." *Detroit News*, March 14, 2015.

Lyons, Mickey. "Macomb's Irish Legacy." *Hour Detroit Magazine*, March 2015.

Mackinac County, Michigan. "Mackinac Island." www.mackinaccounty.net.

Mallory, Dorothy. Interview by Patrick Commins and Elizabeth Rice, 2018.

McDonald, Sean, and Christina Hunt, Christina. "Egan Families of Benzie, Manistee, & Grand Traverse Counties." Michigan Genealogy, www.migenweb.org.

McGee, Reverend John Whalen, and Reverend Richard E. Cross, compilers. *St. Patrick's Church, Irishtown, Michigan 1868–1948, 1898–1948*. Irishtown, MI: Jubilee Journal, 1968.

McRae, Shannon. *Manistee County*. Charleston, SC: Arcadia Publishing, 2006.

Memorial Record of Northern Peninsula of Michigan. Chicago: The Lewis Publishing Company, 1895.

Michigan.gov. "Michigan's Railroad History, 1825–2014." www.michigan.gov.

Michigan State Grange Records, 1873–2009. Michigan State Archives and Historical Collections. East Lansing, Michigan.

Michigan State University. "History of Michigan State University." www.archives.msu.edu.

"Michigan's White Pine Era, 1840–1900." *Michigan History Magazine*, December 1959.

Michigan Tech. "Calumet and Hecla Mining Company." www.mtu.edu/library/archives.

Micketti, Gerald, and Mark Thompson. *Presque Isle: Almost an Island*. Rogers City, MI: Presque Isle County Historical Museum, 2015.

Mindat. "Victoria Mine." www.mindat.org.

Moore, Charles. *History of Michigan*. Chicago: Lewis Publishing Company, 1915.

National Grange of the Order of Patrons of Husbandry. "Mission and Vision." nationalgrange.org.

———. "Our Roots." nationalgrange.org.

National Historic Cheesemaking Center. "The History of Making Cheese." www.nationalhistoriccheesemakingcenter.org.

New World Encyclopedia. "History of the City of Denver, Colorado." www.newworldencyclopedia.org.

Oakland County, Michigan. "Early Oakland County." www.oaklandweb.com.

Owosso Argus Press. "The Kings." June 4, 1957.

Parker, Robert Dale. *The Sound the Stars Make Rushing Through the Sky: The Writings of Jane Johnston Schoolcraft*. Philadelphia: University of Pennsylvania Press, 2008.

Paul, Thomas, MD. "The History of Wayne State University School of Medicine." Plum Health sesquicentennial celebration presentation, plumhealthdpc.com.

Pere Marquette Historical Society. "The Pere Marquette Railroad." www.pmhistsoc.org.

Perry, Kathryn Davarn. *Genealogy of the Families of Fred B. Perry and Kathryn Anne Davarn, His Wife*. N.p: privately printed, 1979.

BIBLIOGRAPHY

"Pioneers of Iosco County, Biography No 2 'Thomas Glendon.'" *Gazette Newspaper*, February 1911.

Portrait and Biographical Album of Barry and Eaton Counties, Michigan. Chicago: Chapman Brothers, 1891.

Portrait and Biographical Album of Branch County, Michigan. Chicago: Chapman Brothers, 1888.

Portrait and Biographical Album of Calhoun County, Michigan. Chicago: Chapman Brothers, 1891.

Portrait and Biographical Album of Clinton and Shiawassee Counties. Chicago: Chapman Brothers, 1894.

Portrait and Biographical Album of Genesee, Lapeer and Tuscola Counties, Michigan. Chicago: Chapman Brothers, 1892.

Portrait and Biographical Album of Hillsdale County, Michigan. Chicago: Chapman Brothers, 1888.

Portrait and Biographical Album of Ingham and Livingston Counties, Michigan. Chicago: Chapman Brothers, 1891.

Portrait and Biographical Album of Isabella County, Michigan. Chicago: Chapman Brothers, 1884.

Portrait and Biographical Album of Jackson County, Michigan. Chicago: Chapman Brothers, 1890.

Portrait and Biographical Album of Lapeer County. Chicago: Chapman Brothers, 1892.

Portrait and Biographical Album of Mecosta County, Michigan. Chicago: Chapman Brothers, 1883.

Portrait and Biographical Album of Newaygo County, Michigan. Chicago: Chapman Brothers, 1884.

Portrait and Biographical Album of Sanilac County. Chicago: Chapman Brothers, 1884.

Portrait and Biographical Album of St. Joseph County, Michigan. Chicago: Chapman Brothers, 1889.

Portrait and Biographical Album of Washtenaw County, Michigan. Chicago: Biographical Publishing Company, 1891.

Portrait and Biographical Record of Berrien and Cass Counties, Michigan. Chicago: Biographical Publishing, 1893.

Portrait and Biographical Record of Kalamazoo, Allegan and Van Buren Counties, Michigan. Chicago: Chapman Brothers, 1892.

Portrait and Biographical Record of Midland County. Chicago: Chapman Brothers, 1884.

Portrait and Biographical Record of Muskegon and Ottawa Counties. Chicago: Biographical Publishing Company, 1893.

Portrait and Biographical Record of Northern Michigan. Chicago: Record Publishing Company, 1895.

Portrait and Biographical Record of Osceola County. Chicago: Chapman Brothers, 1884.

Portrait and Biographical Record of Saginaw and Bay Counties, Michigan. Chicago: Chicago Biographical Publishing Company, 1892.

Portrait and Biographical Sketches of Lenawee County. Chicago: Chapman Brothers, 1888.

Powers, Perry. *History of Northern Michigan.* Chicago: Lewis Publishing Company, 1912.

Prescott, R.E. 1934. *Historic Tales of the Huron Shore Region, and Rhymes.* Vol. 1. Alcona, MI: Alcona County Herald, 1934.

Presque Isle Lighthouse Anniversary. Presque Isle, MI: Presque Isle Township Museum Society, 2015.

Reimann, Lewis. *Between the Iron and the Pine.* Ann Arbor, MI: Edwards Brothers, 1951.

Rice, Denise McCartney. Interview by Patrick Commins and Elizabeth Rice, 2006.

Rice, Dr. Jane, family historian for the McCartney family descendants. Interview by Patrick Commins and Elizabeth Rice, 2019.

Rimer, Julie. "The Strangling Angel of Children." Cemetery Index, www.CemeteryIndex.com.

Roman Catholic Diocese of Marquette. "Bishop Baraga." www.dioceseofmarquette.org.

Rowland, O.W. *A History of Van Buren County, Michigan.* Chicago: Lewis Publishing Company, 1912.

Sawyer, Alvah L. *A History of the Northern Peninsula of Michigan and Its People.* Chicago: Lewis Publishing Company, 1911.

Schaetzl, Randall. "Menominee Iron Range." Department of Geography, Environment, and Spatial Sciences at Michigan State University, www.geo.msu.edu.

———. "The Ontonagon Boulder." Department of Geography, Environment, and Spatial Sciences at Michigan State University, www.geo.msu.edu.

Sharlow, Carrie. "Merrie Hoover Abbott: Michigan Lawyers in History." *Michigan Bar Journal* 97, no. 5 (2018).

Soldiers' and Citizens' Album of Biographical Record of Wisconsin. Chicago: Grand Army Publishing Company, 1888.

Souders, Mrs. Harry, Wedge, Mrs. Ray. *Grayling and Crawford County: History and Miscellaneous. A History of Grayling and Crawford County.* Grayling, MI: Compiled for the Crawford County Library. Grayling, Michigan, 1971.

Southwest Michigan Business and Tourism Directory. "History of Cass County." www.swmidirectory.org.

Teaching History. "Silverites, Populists, and the Movement for Free Silver." www.teachinghistory.org.

Teelander, Alan. "Early Images of the History of Alpena County." Images of Michigan, www.imagesofmichigan.com.

Tozer, James R. *Glen Arbor Pioneers: John LaRau, John Dorsey, John Fisher.* Glen Arbor, MI: Leelanau Press, 2003.

The Traverse Region, Historical and Descriptive: With Illustrations of Scenery. Chicago: H.R. Page & Company, 1884.

Twin Township Library and Historical Society. "The Kings of Irish Settlement." *Twin Township Tales*, 1991.

Upper Peninsula Region of Library Cooperation. www.newspapers.uproc.lib.mi.us.

U.S. Census Agricultural Schedules. www.familysearch.org.

U.S. National Park Service. "Spanish American War—A Splendid Little War." www.nps.gov.

U.S. Postal Service. www.about.usps.com.

Village of Hastings, Ontario. "The History of Hastings, Ontario." www.hastingsvillage.ca.

Wagner, D. The *Poorhouse: America's Forgotten Institution*. Lanham, MD: Rowman-Littlefield Publishers, 2005.

Walbecq, Rebecca. "George Faught." Genealogist on a Journey, www.genealogistonajourney.net.

Wexford County, Michigan. "History of Wexford County." www.wexfordcountyhistory.org.

Wilson, S.J. *Annual Report of the Michigan Dairyman's Association*. Lansing, MI: Wynkoop, Hallenbeck, Crawford Company, 1904.

ABOUT THE AUTHORS

PAT COMMINS was born in Ardee, County Louth, Ireland. He is a retired teacher and administrator who studied at St. Mary's College, Strawberry Hill, Twickenham, London and University College Dublin. Pat has traveled widely throughout his career. He is a student of Irish history, which he has shared through many presentations given to various groups in Michigan. Pat lives in Dublin, Ireland.

ELIZABETH RICE is a retired teacher who lives in Michigan. Elizabeth graduated with a bachelor of arts degree from Albion College. She earned a master's degree from the University of Michigan. She has a keen interest in people and their stories. Elizabeth listened to family stories from a young age, which inspired her to become a writer. She is captivated by learning life lessons from simple experiences, people she meets, nature and unexpected encounters.